Should We Stay Together?

Should We Stay Together?

A SCIENTIFICALLY PROVEN METHOD
FOR EVALUATING YOUR RELATIONSHIP
AND IMPROVING ITS CHANCES FOR LONG-TERM SUCCESS

Jeffry H. Larson, Ph.D.

Foreword by Robert F. Stahmann, Ph.D.

 JOSSEY-BASS
A Wiley Company
San Francisco

Jossey-Bass books and products are available through most bookstores. To contact Jossey-Bass directly, call (888) 378-2537, fax to (800) 605-2665, or visit our website at www.josseybass.com.

Substantial discounts on bulk quantities of Jossey-Bass books are available to corporations, professional associations, and other organizations. For details and discount information, contact the special sales department at Jossey-Bass.

Manufactured in the United States of America on Lyons Falls Turin Book. This paper is acid-free and 100 percent totally chlorine-free.

Library of Congress Cataloging-in-Publication Data
Larson, Jeffry H.
   Should we stay together? : a scientifically proven method for evaluating your relationship and improving its chances for long-term success / Jeffry H. Larson ; foreword by Robert F. Stahmann.
        p.   cm.
Includes bibliographical references.
   ISBN 0-7879-5144-7 (pbk. : alk. paper)
   1. Mate selection. 2. Marriage compatibility tests. I. Title.
   HQ801 .L299 2000
   306.81—dc21   99-050745

FIRST EDITION

PB Printing   10 9 8 7 6 5 4 3

Contents

To my children,

Geoffrey, Dillon, Tyler, and Hallie.

May the concepts in this book help guide you to satisfying marriages.

Foreword

The fact that you have picked up this book and are reading these pages probably indicates your interest in understanding and predicting marital satisfaction. Whether you are contemplating marriage soon, looking at it as a future happening, or looking back at your current marriage to see what you "should have known," this book will be very useful to you. It will give you information, questions, ideas, stories, and concepts to study and ponder so that you can make a better decision about when and whom to marry.

The information and insights contained in *Should We Stay Together?* are based on sound research and clinical knowledge. The book content is solid and well-founded, and the style of presenting the information is engaging and very "reader friendly."

I have been involved in writing and teaching premarital counseling for over thirty years. I have known Jeffry Larson and his work for some fifteen years. He and I share a common professional interest in premarital counseling and education—in marriage preparation. As I attend professional meetings and read our professional and scientific literature, Dr. Larson is one of the leaders in presenting and writing about marriage preparation. He is a highly respected scholar. Dr. Larson is actively involved in doing research and providing premarital counseling. While this background and activity adds to our field, for you the reader, his knowledge, credibility, and sensitivity come through in his writing of this book for you.

Should We Stay Together? is a book that is based on the best of what is known about predicting and understanding marital satisfaction. The style and content are unique and usefully presented so as to be directly applicable to couples, by couples themselves. For example, the "Marriage Triangle," an easily understood device, is presented as a means of discovering the importance of individual traits, couple traits, and the context in which the couple lives and functions. Questions and answers from the RELATE premarital inventory are included, which also aid in self- and couple evaluation of the relationship. What do you believe about reasons to marry? A discussion of popular marital myths will cause you to ponder these socially accepted ideas and sort out your own beliefs as you evaluate your marriage reasoning and readiness.

A primary strength of the book is the inclusion of numerous exercises and examples that can involve the reader in self- and couple interaction and dialogue. I encourage you to become involved with your prospective spouse in reading and responding to the book content. By doing so, the two of you will avail yourselves of crucial material that can enhance your likelihood of marital satisfaction. You will then be able to say, "I'm glad that I know that," rather than "If only I had known!"

Robert F. Stahmann, Ph.D.
Author, *Premarital and Remarital Counseling*

Acknowledgments

I want to thank several people for their support of this work and the preparation of the manuscript. Thanks to Dr. Tom Holman, a dear colleague and friend who shares my passion for discovering the premarital predictors of marital satisfaction and then communicating research findings to the audience that really needs to know them: single adults. Tom is a masterful researcher and writer. Thanks to another colleague, Dr. Alan Hawkins, director of the Family Studies Center at Brigham Young University, for his financial contribution to this project and consistent encouragement of me. Thanks to Alan Rinzler, executive editor at Jossey-Bass, for his editing and good suggestions on how to make the manuscript more complete and concise. Finally, love and thanks to my wife, Jeannie, who edited and typed the manuscript in a professional and timely manner.

February 2000   J.H.L.

Introduction

Sandy and Charles met two months ago. It seemed like instant love. They really felt connected from the first night, when they stayed up until 4 A.M. sharing their backgrounds and experiences. There seemed to be almost an instant rapport between them—almost like they had known each other forever.

Sandy and Charles found themselves spending most of their free time together when they were not at work or attending the local university. They became increasingly intimate with each other both emotionally and sexually. This fast-track romance worried both sets of parents, who lived in the same community. Sandy was only eighteen while Charles was twenty-five. Sandy's parents worried that Charles was just taking advantage of their young, naive daughter— "He probably only wants an easy sexual relationship," they said. Charles's family did not approve of Sandy from day one. Charles's mother was offended with Sandy's direct but sometimes offensive style of communication. She also thought Sandy was "not good enough" for her son.

Charles and Sandy felt almost like Romeo and Juliet—passionately in love but with no parental approval of their relationship. Both also worried that if the passion continued, they might break their own shared moral code not to have sexual intercourse before marriage, which would also invite more disapproval from their conservative parents and friends and complicate the situation even more. Each day they pondered what to do next. Marriage was their goal, but when? And how should they respond to so much parental disapproval?

Sandy had read that women who marry under the age of twenty have higher divorce rates than those who are older, but assured herself that she and Charles would be an exception. What she wanted most now was to prove to herself and her parents that this was a good idea—to marry Charles in the next few months. She searched diligently for a way to prove that they were well-matched, mature enough to marry, and had the traits that are related to future marital satisfaction, both as individuals and as a couple.

At this point I met Sandy and Charles, and directed them to the comprehensive premarital assessment questions found in this book. I knew that these questions would help them determine their readiness for marriage, since they came from a comprehensive premarital assessment questionnaire called the RELATionship Evaluation (RELATE).[1] I advised them to answer the questions in this book, score each short test, and discuss their findings with me and then with their parents. I hoped that this approach would make all the parties in this situation calmer and more rational.

Trent (thirty), and Monica (twenty-eight) were in a very different situation. They had known each other for over five years and had spent the last two years living together. They strongly believed that living together would help them better understand what it was really like to be married without the fear of rushing into a permanent relationship.

Trent's parents had a messy divorce when he was only ten years old, and Monica's parents, although still married, had more of a roommate arrangement than a marriage. Monica's mother repeatedly warned Monica to be very careful in choosing someone to marry—"You don't want to spend all of your life taking care of some man like I have," she warned. So, being very anxious about marriage, Trent and Monica felt that getting to know each other better and experimenting with what it is like to be married was the best approach to take in their relationship at this time.

Unfortunately, both of them really wanted to be married. They wondered how long they should continue to "prove the relationship will work." Their family backgrounds worried both of them. Would they, too, be doomed to eventual divorce? Does divorce run in families? Neither set of parents had good communication or conflict resolution skills. Were their skills adequate for marriage? More broadly, what are the factors that predict if they would be happily married? Where does one find such information?

These were some of the many questions Trent and Monica asked when we met for the first time. They wanted both accurate information and a way to assess their unique situation. The material in this book provided them with both.

The Beatles sang, "All you need is love." Your teacher might tell you, "Good communication is all you *really* need." Your parents may advise you, "The key is, marry someone with the same values." Everyone has advice for single people considering marriage. The problem is, none of this advice is totally correct, nor is it totally incorrect.

So what premarital factors best predict the future success of your marriage? What kinds of couples should not get married? What types of individuals should you avoid as your future spouse? How do you know when you are not ready to marry? If you are in a serious relationship currently, should you pursue marriage, break up, or just keep dating? With the divorce rate in the United States approaching 50 percent of the marriages entered into today, it's no wonder people are anxious about marriage and asking these kinds of questions.

Another source of confusion are the myths about mate selection and preparing for marriage that we pick up from popular magazines, television soap operas, movies, peers, and even our own relatives. Our acceptance of such myths is a result of misleading information about the nature of marriage and preparation for marriage, misinterpretations of correct information, and inferences made from our own limited experiences. As we'll see in Chapter One, such myths include "Love is enough," "Living together will prepare us for marriage," and "Preparing for marriage comes naturally." The problem is, where do you get valid and reliable information about the predictors of marital satisfaction? Do the talk-show hosts or radio personalities know what predicts a successful marriage? Will Ann Landers help? What about the self-help books written by pop psychologists or popular lecture circuit speakers?

This is a book about preparing for marriage, but it's very different from the typical self-help publications on this topic in several important ways. First, I am not a pop psychologist with my own biased set of ideas on what predicts marital satisfaction. Instead, I am a researcher and therapist at a major university with twenty years of experience in researching the scientific literature and conducting my own research on premarital predictors. Using a comprehensive review of the literature and our most recent and original research using a new scientific questionnaire called RELATE, I can provide you with the latest information on the factors and issues that will help determine whom and when to marry. As you read this book you, too, will have the opportunity to take the most important parts of the RELATE test to obtain expert guidance for your own situation.

This book was written for single individuals and couples interested in improving their chances of being happily married *before* marriage, but it can also be helpful to married couples who are wondering what went wrong or whether to make a fresh start—together or separately. It can be read alone or with a partner. It can be read by itself or alongside a traditional college marriage and family textbook. It can be used in a marriage preparation workshop in a church or secular setting. Wherever you are, it will increase your chances of marital success if you make use of the guidelines herein.

Where the Research Came From

Over the last ten years, family scientist Dr. Tom Holman and I have done an exhaustive review of the social science research literature on premarital characteristics that predict later marital satisfaction. In reviewing clinical and research literature from about 1935 to the present, we found over two dozen specifics that contribute to marital satisfaction. We grouped these characteristics (for example, age at marriage or degree of acquaintance) into three general, major factors: context, individual traits, and couple traits). These three major factors make up the Marriage Triangle described later in this book. In the last three years we conducted new longitudinal research on the premarital predictors in the Marriage Triangle and developed the questionnaire titled RELATE. This recent research verified and clarified the importance of each of the three major factors in the triangle and the multiple subfactors in each dimension in the prediction of marital satisfaction. The validity and reliability of the RELATE questionnaire has also been verified.

In addition to my research, it has been my clinical observation that many couples in marital therapy trace their current marriage problems back to the premarital relationship or circumstances surrounding the marriage (for example, feeling pressured to marry, dealing with a premarital pregnancy, and so on). It seems that many couples get off to a bad start right from the beginning. It's as though some marriages are doomed before they even start. Hence, my desire in this book is to help you avoid or solve problems *before* you marry by informing you of the premarital predictors of marital satisfaction, helping you assess your strengths and weaknesses as an individual and a couple and make better decisions about whom to marry and when to marry.

I recognize that premarital factors alone cannot predict a marriage future. Many stressors or enhancers of marital satisfaction occur after months or years of marriage. For example, the birth of a child puts both positive and negative stress on a marriage that can affect marital satisfaction. However, I believe that it is important for all couples to begin their marriages with the most resources and the fewest hardships possible. This way, initial adjustments to married life will be smoother and future stressors should be easier to cope with.

The Purpose of This Book

This book will introduce you to the factors that research shows predict a successful first marriage. It will help you assess these factors in your own life and relationship, and help you apply your new self- and couple knowledge to your current and future relationships.

More specifically, this book will help you with these key insights and decision points:

- Understand your personal assets and liabilities as a potential spouse. I call this your *marriage aptitude.*
- Evaluate your relationship's assets and liabilities.
- Evaluate the contexts of your relationship, e.g., parental and friends' approval.
- Set goals for personal and couple development so you are better prepared for marriage.
- Decide whom to marry and when to marry.
- Find high-quality resources to help you prepare for marriage.

In this book I have included only the premarital predictors that have been consistently supported in the research literature. When there are inconsistent or contradictory findings, I report the findings that I believe are most representative of the literature as a whole.

Chapter One begins with a description of the popular myths in our society about preparing for marriage—including the most dangerous one: "We know practically nothing about what predicts a happy marriage." Chapter Two introduces you to the three major premarital predictors of marital satisfaction—contexts, individual traits, and couple traits—that form what I call the *Marriage Triangle*. I also introduce you to how you will assess these factors in your own life using short tests found in each chapter. Chapters Three through Five describe each of the three factors in the triangle in more depth. Each chapter concludes with interpretation guidelines for your personal assessments, questions to consider and discuss, and suggestions on how to improve your preparation for marriage based on each factor in the triangle. A summary of your personal assessments and their meanings occurs in Chapter Six. This gives you an opportunity to inventory your assets and liabilities and set goals for personal and couple development so you are better prepared for marriage. Chapter Seven is different from the other chapters in that it serves as a warning—my last piece of advice as to certain kinds of people (for example, verbally abusive individuals) you should avoid marrying (whom not to marry), and situations or circumstances (for example, you're both teenagers) that indicate you should not marry (when not to marry). Finally, Chapter Eight contains descriptions of other high-quality premarital resources including books, training programs, and organizations that will increase your personal and couple readiness for marriage.

Now let's get back to the two couples introduced earlier in this introduction. First, what happened to Sandy and Charles? We discussed their results from taking the RELATE and discovered several "red lights." These included young age (she was eighteen), a lack of sufficient acquaintance, parental disapproval, dysfunctional families of origin, parental divorce and dissatisfaction, intimidation by their parents, a lack of career or financial resources to support marriage, problems with Charles's ability to share his feelings, a lack of conflict resolution skills in their relationship, and Charles's internal pressure to get married soon.

When Sandy and Charles participated in the premarital assessment process with me, they realized that these ten red lights had largely gone unnoticed in their relationship—and they had minimized and denied the ones they did notice. Consequently, they decided to postpone marriage, get to know each other better, finish more of their education and career development, and get better acquainted with their future in-laws. I congratulated them and encouraged them that as a result, their future in-laws would most likely become more accepting of them as individuals and more supportive of their eventual marriage. Two years later I received a wedding announcement from Sandy. She attached a note explaining how different things were as a result of dealing directly with these red lights. Their in-laws had come round to support (or at least not oppose) their marriage, they were more financially and emotionally ready for marriage, and their couple communication skills had improved.

Trent and Monica also learned much from learning about the concepts and techniques and completing the assessments that you will find in this book. Red lights for this couple included dysfunctional marriages in both families of origin and a traumatizing parental divorce in Trent's family. Trent also admitted being a survivor of childhood emotional and physical abuse. These traumatic experiences caused Monica and especially Trent to feel very anxious about marriage. Commitment was especially a problem for both of them. They wondered how they could ensure that divorce would not affect them, too, later. They were living together hoping to prove the relationship would work before moving on to marriage. It was like a trial marriage for them. But their conflict resolution style was to avoid conflict rather than deal with the issues. They were so anxious about making waves in the relationship that they never directly confronted serious disagreements. Instead, both of them swept conflict under the carpet. Naturally, the carpet was getting lumpy and they were beginning to trip over it frequently! It became obvious to them that they needed counseling to develop conflict resolution skills and reduce anxiety reduction before thinking more seriously about marriage. As a result of counseling they decided to break up but continue working in therapy on the personal issues that were getting in the way of forming a lasting relationship.

It is my hope that as a result of reading this book and assessing yourself and your relationship you will be better prepared, less anxious, and make a better decision about whom and when to marry—and that all of this will result in many years of satisfying life together.

ONE

Myths About Preparing for Marriage

The high divorce rate in the United Sates and the resulting concern with marrying the right person makes selecting someone to marry an especially important contemporary issue. You may struggle with finding the right person to marry, feeling competent as a future spouse, or feeling confident that a relationship will work. This is partly due to the magnitude of the decision, the increasingly high expectations we have of marriage (for example, "My spouse should simultaneously be my lover, my best friend, and my counselor"), and the fact that if you do not choose carefully, the marriage could end in divorce.

Myths: What Are They?

A significant cause of your struggle with the decision may be your belief in myths about selecting a mate and preparing for marriage. Myths are widely held beliefs that are not true. That is, there is no scientific evidence to support them, yet many people believe them.

To assess your belief in the myths about preparing for marriage, rate how much you agree or disagree with each of the statements in Exhibit 1.1.

For each of the myths you agreed with, think of your reasoning in support of the myth. For example, who taught you this myth? What evidence do you have that this myth is true? False? Your belief-in-myths score is high if you agreed or strongly

	Circle your responses:				
	Strongly Disagree	*Disagree*	*Undecided*	*Agree*	*Strongly Agree*
1. There is one and only one right person in the world for you to marry.	1	2	3	4	5
2. Until a person finds the perfect person to marry, he or she should not be satisfied.	1	2	3	4	5
3. You should feel totally competent as a future spouse before you decide to get married.	1	2	3	4	5
4. You can be happy with anyone you choose to marry if you try hard enough.	1	2	3	4	5
5. You should choose someone to marry whose personal characteristics are opposite from your own.	1	2	3	4	5
6. Being in love with someone is sufficient reason to marry that person.	1	2	3	4	5
7. Choosing someone to marry is a "decision of the heart."	1	2	3	4	5
8. Living together will prepare you for marriage and improve your chances of being happily married.	1	2	3	4	5
9. Choosing a mate should be easy.	1	2	3	4	5
10. Preparing for marriage "just comes naturally."	1	2	3	4	5
11. We know practically nothing about what predicts a happy marriage, so just take your chances.	1	2	3	4	5

For which myths did you circle "Agree" or "Strongly Agree"? Write these myths in the spaces given here.

1._____

2._____

3._____

4._____

5._____

Exhibit 1.1. Preparation for Modern Marriage—The Myths

agreed with five or more of the myths. If you agreed or strongly agreed with three or four myths, your score is moderate. Agreeing with two or fewer is a low myth score. The more myths you marked "Uncertain" to "Strongly Disagree," the better your understanding of the true nature of selecting someone to marry and preparing for marriage.

Myths such as these are dangerous because they may lead you to be too critical or not critical enough—of yourself, your partner, your relationship, or your decision about marriage. They may also lead you to seek the wrong kind of person to marry. They may set up irrational expectations, such as "choosing someone to marry is easy." They may fool you into believing that you and your spouse will live happily ever after—regardless of your incompatibilities.

The most disturbing myth is the one that says, "We know practically nothing about the factors that predict a happy marriage." This book was written to debunk the whole set of myths but especially this one, and educate you about the premarital predictors of marriage satisfaction based on over half a century of research.

ଞ Debunking the Myths

Let's go into more detail on these eleven myths about preparing for marriage. We'll see why each myth is false and provide an alternative, more realistic belief for each myth. I believe that if you can rid yourself of your belief in these myths and start thinking more realistically about preparing for marriage, you will have taken the first step toward a more satisfying, healthier, and ultimately easier experience in preparing for marriage. The first two myths concern your partner.

You're My One and Only

The myth: *There is one and only one right person in the world for you to marry.*

Expect several negative consequences if you endorse this belief. For example, how do you determine when you have found this one right person? Will you experience a special, even magical feeling? Will you pass up other good marriage prospects while waiting for this special feeling?

Such a belief may also foster passivity in selecting someone to marry. For example, if you believe that your "one and only" will eventually just come along, there will be no positive pressure to date actively and get to know others more intimately. This was the case for a college student I once counseled. He argued that the person he should marry would be revealed to him by God and that until he received such a revelation, he saw no reason to spend his time and money dating multiple partners. I argued that God helps those who help themselves!

There is no scientific evidence that there is one and only one best person in the world for any individual to marry. If this myth were true, why would people remarry after the death of a beloved spouse?

The reality: *There are several individuals to whom you could be happily married.*

The fact that there is no "one and only" in no way militates against using good judgment when selecting a spouse. Rather, it means that if one person does not measure up—assuming your standards are realistic in terms of your own assets—there are other persons who will.

The Perfect Partner

The myth: *Until a person finds the perfect person to marry, he or she should not be satisfied.*

This is an unrealistic expectation. Such a desire for perfection reduces your ability to find solutions, and can lead to the opposite of your desired results. We live in a world of probabilities. The desire for absolute truth and security leads to exaggerated expectations that cannot be fulfilled and consequently produces indecisiveness and anxiety in the mate selection process.[1]

If you believe there is a perfect partner for you somewhere out there, you will be likely to engage in short-term "rating relationships" in order to more quickly identify if a person is Mr. or Miss Perfect. After all, who wants to waste their time dating someone with whom there is no future? Instead of getting to know your dates and relating to them, you will instead evaluate and *rate them*—prematurely. You will then develop a pattern of multiple short-term relationships, which lead to frustration, disappointment, and disillusionment for both you and your dating partners. The pointlessness of this belief is further amplified by the fact that people change over time. The person who appeared perfect at the beginning of the relationship will inevitably appear imperfect later.[2]

This frustrating pattern was described to be by Rhonda (thirty-six), a single, attractive woman who was a colleague of mine. When I first met her and found out she had never married, I was shocked. One day at lunch I discovered why. She described her search for the "perfect guy"!! This was fueled by her irrational belief that she must not make a mistake—that would be shameful! She reported having been engaged three times in the last five years, only to break off each engagement about thirty days before the wedding. She was paralyzed with the belief that there was a perfect partner somewhere out there. The closer she got to the wedding day, the more worried she was that this guy might not be perfect. She was about resigned to being single for life. I emphasized the self-defeating nature of her perfection and shame beliefs. She later thanked me for helping her confront her problem.

The reality: *No one is perfect.*

Select a mate based on the qualities that are most important to you, and be able to compromise when all the qualities are not found. A balance sheet with the pluses and minuses of a particular relationship may be useful for you. The most you can hope for is to decide in light of the best information available.

The next two myths focus on *you.*

The Perfect Self

The myth: *You should feel totally competent as a future spouse before you decide to get married.*

This belief will keep you single for a long time, because few individuals ever feel totally competent to be a husband or a wife. In addition, successful marriage requires cooperation and effort by two people, not perfection in one or both. You may use this belief as a rationalization for an underlying fear of close relationships or marriage.

A thirty-one-year-old man I know used this excuse to remain single. He attended nearly every self-improvement seminar that rolled into town. He constantly read magazines promising to provide the eternal truths: "What women *really* want in their lover," and "How to talk to women so they will find you irresistible." This guy ended up with enough self-esteem and phony lines for five men! Friends inadvertently reinforced this belief about competency by praising him for such devotion to self-improvement. I questioned his real motive and he later disclosed that he had once been engaged and his fiancée was untrue. He was devastated! He swore he would never let another woman take advantage of him!

The reality: *A person should feel competent to be a spouse, though some feelings of anxiety are natural.*

However, this anxiety should not keep you from marrying. No one is perfect, and no one can perfectly predict the future adjustments a couple will have to make.

Just Try Harder

The myth: *You can be happy with anyone you choose to marry if you try hard enough.*

This is the opposite of the perfect partner belief. The negative consequences include taking a too casual approach to mate selection (since "just about anyone will do"), fostering another unrealistic belief that "with enough effort anything is possible," and premature marriage (that is, committing to a relationship before carefully evaluating similarities, differences, values, goals, expectations, and so on). The truth is, some people I have counseled have such serious personality or behavioral problems that just about anyone would go crazy trying to live with them!

A good example of this kind of person is one who has very low self-esteem and little confidence. This person is overly dependent on a partner for attention and love. Recently a man engaged to such a woman resentfully described how she followed him around "like a puppy dog." "Day and night, Dr. Larson, she demands my undivided attention. I can't even go study for a few hours without her resenting it, guilt-tripping me for being gone so long, and accusing me of not putting her first in my life. Nothing I do is ever enough!" This poor guy was not only frustrated but significantly depressed over this situation. He was not sleeping, eating, or concentrating well. He was in danger of flunking out of school in his last semester as an MBA student.

People with active addictions to alcohol, drugs, sex, work, or whatever are another example of individuals who are nearly impossible to live with happily. And all the effort on the spouse's part seldom results in the addict's changing or the relationship's improving significantly. As they say, addicts usually have to bottom out before they will seriously change. Bottoming out will probably include destroying the relationship first.

Many married individuals who hold this try-hard-enough belief have experienced months or years of "trying harder" to make the marriage work without much success. This is because marriage is a reciprocal relationship that requires both spouses' working together to resolve relationship problems.

The reality: *It takes two mature and well-adjusted individuals to make a marriage work, so one needs to be reasonably sensitive and selective in the choice of a mate.*

A prospective mate should be someone who is willing to give their fair share to the relationship, to compromise, and to be sensitive to equity in the relationship.[3]

Opposites Improve Marriage

The myth: *You should choose someone to marry whose personal characteristics are opposite from your own.*

Unfortunately, this belief encourages you to look for partners who are different from rather than similar to yourself. It also encourages irresponsibility on your part (for example, the sloppy person who marries the neat person, thinking that the neat person will pick up after him or her), and it discourages personal change (for example, rather than changing your shortcomings, you find someone who is the opposite of you and who you think will make up for your shortcomings).

Although in some cases opposites may attract, marrying someone whose traits are significantly different from your own will probably lead to conflict and dissatisfaction.

When Jason—an impulsive spender—met Mary, he was attracted to her self-control and thriftiness. He thought she would be a good complement to him if they married. She would keep his spending sprees under control! After less than two years of marriage his label of her as "thrifty" had evolved into "stingy"! They even fought about money on their honeymoon!

The reality: *A person should choose someone to marry whose personal characteristics are similar to his or her own.* "Polar opposites may find one another enjoyable, different, and alluring for a limited time. However, long-term relationships usually flourish when similarity rather than dissimilarity prevails."[4]

The next five myths concern the process of selecting someone to marry and preparing for marriage.

Love Is Enough

The myth: *Being in love with someone is sufficient reason to marry that person.*

Simply because you are profoundly attracted to a person and have passionate feelings of love does not mean for a moment that you should marry that person! Falling in love is easy. Marriage based mostly on emotion or hormones rather than reason is dangerous. Premarital relationships based mostly on these factors often result in premature marriages before people really know each other well.

Romantic love actually may be something else, for example, a strong sex drive, a flight from loneliness, a neurotic attachment (as in the case of an over-adequate partner married to an under-adequate partner), or an excuse for domination and control. "The expression 'I love you' has such immutable place in our traditions that it can serve as an excuse for anything, even for selfishness and evil."[5] The irrational strength of some individuals' belief in this myth is exemplified by a couple I saw in a premarital counseling session. The woman sat in a session with her admitted drug-addicted fiancé and spoke about how important it was to her for him to provide her with emotional and financial support when they married. Knowing this emotionally unstable and chronically unemployed man well, I asked how she expected him to do this. After all, wouldn't she more likely end up taking care of him, instead? In response to this question she smiled and commented, "But, Dr. Larson, you don't understand. I *love* him." My thought at this expression was, "So what?"

Although romantic love is a requisite for marriage for most American couples, marital success is based on many other important factors as well, including similarity of values, similarity of backgrounds, age at marriage, personal and couple readiness for marriage, realistic expectations, and happy childhood. Of the two dozen or so premarital predictors related to marital satisfaction as determined by researchers, romantic love is only one.

The reality: *Although romantic love is important, especially in the early stage of a relationship, other factors are equally or more important to marital satisfaction and should be considered before marriage.*

A Decision of the Heart

The myth: *Choosing someone to marry is a "decision of the heart."*

This reflects an underlying belief that the ultimate decision of marriage should be based on feelings rather than thought. Some people trust their feelings over their thinking processes. Unfortunately, there is no scientific evidence that making a marriage decision based solely on feelings is wise. In fact, it is unwise! True peace of mind about marrying a person comes from not only feeling this is the right thing to do, but also knowing on a more rational, analytical level that this is the right thing to do.

On one occasion, I suggested this concept to a student in my marriage preparation class. She exclaimed, "I know realistically that Tom and I are very different from each other. He is from another race, religion, and cultural group. I know the adjustments will be many, but darn it, I love him, and I should follow my heart!" Hearing this, I engaged her in a discussion (focused on thoughts, not feelings) of the many specific adjustments the two of them would have to make to make this marriage work. She had never carefully thought about all these adjustments before. After our cognitive discussion, her heart was less sure of itself! As a result, this couple came to twelve sessions of premarital counseling before they eventually married.

If you are wise you will base your marriage decision on both thoughts and feelings. You should feel good about the decision and, more objectively, you should analyze your decision so that if you explained to me your decision to marry—that is, why your partner is a good choice, why you feel ready, why the relationship and circumstances surrounding it (the context) are favorable—I would see your logic and the wisdom in your decision.

The reality: *Choosing someone to marry is a decision of the heart* and *the head.*

Let's Live Together

The myth: *Living together will prepare you for marriage and improve your chances of being happily married.*

Mounting evidence shows that living together—which scientists call *cohabitation*—is significantly different from marriage and that cohabitation used as a "trial marriage" usually does *not* improve a couple's chances for later marital success. In fact, as you will learn later in Chapter Five, serial cohabitors have higher divorce rates than those who do not cohabit! It turns out that serial cohabitors lack the level of commitment necessary to maintain a long-term marriage. They often distrust themselves or their partners and they tend to be more unconventional about marriage than others. Unconventional attitudes are related to higher divorce rates.

A good example of an unconventional attitude toward marriage was *open marriage*—espoused by some social scientists in the 1970s. In such a marriage, the spouses gave each other permission to have sex with outsiders. This was thought to enrich the marriage and rid it of some of its boredom. The divorce rate for such relationships was so high that social scientists gave up on the idea very quickly—but some prospective spouses still want to give it a try!

The negative consequences of the belief in cohabitation as "marriage insurance" include violating your moral standards and later regretting it, creating tension with your parents if they disapprove, and later feeling disillusioned when cohabitation fails to make the relationship divorce-proof.

The reality: *Cohabitation may help us get to know each other better, but will not serve as a trial marriage or increase our chances of being happily married.*

It's Supposed to Be Easy

The myth: *Choosing a mate should be easy.*

There is a popular belief that marriage and mate selection are a matter of chance. The myth that mate selection is accidental or easy relieves you of the responsibility for failure in a relationship or responsibility for taking action to help a relationship flourish. It also may discourage you from participating in marriage preparation programs and premarital counseling.

The popularity of self-help books, the RELATE and other similar premarital assessment questionnaires, magazine articles on finding a mate, and marriage preparation courses suggests that mate selection may not be as easy as it once was. Experts now warn individuals about poor reasons to get married, people one should not marry, myths about marriage that can damage the relationship, avoiding addictive relationships, and so on. These books and articles focus on not making mistakes before marriage. They contain lists of questions individuals should ask themselves before they marry, including, How well do we communicate and understand each other? How do we usually handle disagreements? and How well do we know each other?

The reality: *Choosing a mate is not easy; the decision should be carefully thought out.*

Our society has undergone rapid changes that confound marriage and career decisions. Changing sex roles, the high divorce rate, the effect of inflation on the family, the need for higher education, and higher expectations for marriage have made choosing a mate and marriage preparation more complicated than fifty years ago.

Marriage Is Instinctive

The myth: *Preparing for marriage "just comes naturally."*

Do you believe marriage does not take any special knowledge or skills? Many people believe the myth that we are born with or somehow magically learn from our parents or peers how to pick a suitable mate and how to prepare for marriage. This is referred to as the *myth of naturalism.*[6] Unfortunately, what you often learn from others about finding a mate or preparing for marriage is either incorrect or limited information.

I'll never forget the day in my university marriage preparation course when a student reported to me what his father said to him when he told him he was taking my course. His father exclaimed, "Why in the world are you taking marriage prep? That stuff just comes naturally—you know, it's part of growing up!" I asked the student how much he actually had learned so far in life about preparing for a satisfying marriage and he responded, "Practically nothing!"

The reality: *Preparing for marriage is learned and is based on sound information and personal assessment.*

So where do you get accurate information and develop the skills necessary to prepare for marriage and make a wise choice? One good source is social science research. The purpose of this book is to give you some of the most important, basic information from social science research that will help you in the process of finding a suitable mate and preparing for marriage. Reading this book and thoughtfully completing the assessments and exercises herein will serve as your first scientific marital preparation. This book is limited to preparing for marriage and selecting a suitable partner. There are many other good books you can read after this one on how to maintain marital satisfaction after the wedding.

Nobody Knows What Will Work

The myth: *We know practically nothing about what predicts a happy marriage, so just take your chances.*

Fortunately, people who believe this myth are *wrong!* Although there is still much to learn about the premarital factors that predict happiness in marriage, my research on this subject and the RELATE questions in this book can tell you very much. This book helps fill the information gap in our society on what predicts a happy marriage.

You may be used to consulting the physical sciences to make good choices—for example, you may read *Consumer Reports* for research on the top ten automobiles before buying one. In a sense, this book is a "social science" version of *Consumer Reports* on marriage preparation. It will inform you about marriage, marriage preparation, selecting a person to marry, and most important, assessing yourself and your relationship.

The reality: *We know many things about the predictors of marital satisfaction that can help you have a happier marriage.*

&8 Moving Beyond the Myths: What We Know

Now let's turn to the subject of what we know. Chapter Two introduces you to the model I call the *Marriage Triangle*—three key premarital factors that predict later marital satisfaction. The remainder of this book explains the specific subfactors in each of these more general factors that predict marital satisfaction. It also gives you the opportunity to assess yourself and your relationship on each of these important points, and to set goals for improvement in your individual and couple marriage readiness. At the end of the book (Chapters Six through Eight) I'll show you how to bring all these factors and your own assessments together to make a better choice of whom to marry and when to marry.

CHAPTER

TWO

The Marriage Triangle

Three Factors That Predict Your Future Marital Satisfaction

After reviewing the premarital prediction literature and conducting our research, we found that the two dozen or so specific premarital predictors could be logically categorized into a triangular model of three major factors:

- Your individual and relationship *contexts*

- Your *individual traits* including your personality, attitudes, and skills

- Your *couple traits,* including couple communication, couple history, similarities, and so on

Figure 2.1 presents these factors in graphic form.

For an introduction to these three factors, first answer the questions in Exhibit 2.1. These are examples of questions from the RELATE instrument that you will also respond to later in Chapters Three through Five.

Items 1–3 measure your perceptions of some of the characteristics in your individual context—the level of affection in your family of origin, your father's marital satisfaction, and your parent-child relationship satisfaction. Your score may range from 3 (lowest) to 15 (highest). This score is a rough indicator of your overall satisfaction with your family-of-origin experiences.

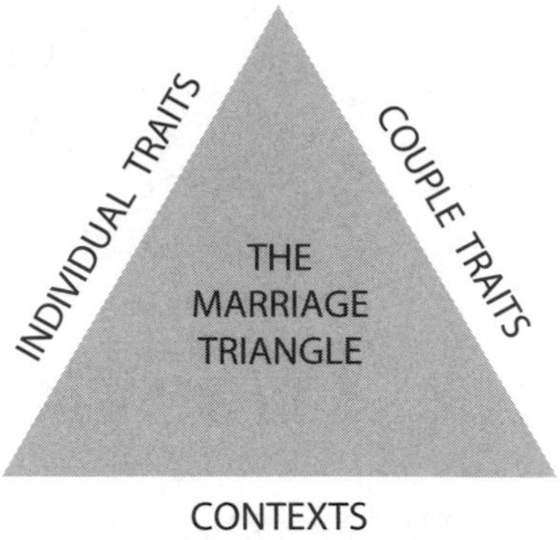

Figure 2.1. The Marriage Triangle

Items 4–6 are measures of your individual traits including self-esteem, anger management, and extroversion. Again, scores may range from 3 to 15 and reflect your perception of your overall mental health.

Items 7–9 are measures of your perceived couple traits, more specifically, communication and problem-solving skills. Scores range from 3 to 15 and reflect the overall quality of your couple communication skills.

A total score below 9 on one of these tests suggests a potential problem in that area of the Marriage Triangle. For example, a total score of 7 on items 7–9 indicates poor couple communication or conflict resolution skills. A score of 11 or more indicates good couple communication or conflict resolution skills. In which area—contexts, individual traits, or couple traits—did you score the highest? The lowest? Why? These questions and scoring guidelines are generalizations because to assess each factor in the triangle comprehensively requires answering more questions from each area in the triangle. You will do that throughout Chapters Three, Four, and Five. These miniature tests are presented now simply as an introduction to the three factors in the triangle. Now, let's look more extensively at each factor.

Personal and Relationship Contexts

Personal context characteristics include family-of-origin influences, such as the degree of cohesion or unity in the family in which you grew up, the quality of your

	Circle your responses:				
	Strongly Disagree	*Disagree*	*Undecided*	*Agree*	*Strongly Agree*
1. My father was happy in his marriage.	1	2	3	4	5
2. All things considered, my childhood years were happy.	1	2	3	4	5
3. My mother showed physical affection to me by appropriate hugging and/or kissing.	1	2	3	4	5
4. I feel I am a person of worth.	1	2	3	4	5
5. I avoid getting irritated or mad.	1	2	3	4	5
6. I am an outgoing person.	1	2	3	4	5
7. We understand each other's feelings.	1	2	3	4	5
8. We sit down and just talk things over.	1	2	3	4	5
9. When we are in an argument, we recognize when we are overwhelmed and then make a deliberate effort to calm ourselves down.	1	2	3	4	5

1. To score these items, sum your responses to items 1–3 and write your answer here: _____

2. Sum your responses to items 4–6 and write your answer here: _____

3. Sum your responses to items 7–9 and write your answer here: _____

Exhibit 2.1. Sample RELATE Questions

parent-child relationships, the quality of your parents' marriage, and your parents' mental health. Other personal context characteristics include your age, education, and socioeconomic status at the time you marry.

Relationship context influences refer to the situation or environment in which you and your relationship exist. Examples of premarital relationship context factors that will affect your later marital satisfaction are parental and friends' approval of your marriage, and internal and external pressures to marry. Internal pressures refer to self-induced pressures to get married (for example, many women over thirty feel they should be married by that age). External pressures come from your environment (for example, parental pressure for grandchildren). These pressures may result in your marrying before you are ready.

Personal and relationship contexts are purposely placed at the base or foundation of the Marriage Triangle. This is because your experiences in your family of origin and your continuing relationship with your parents form the basis or foundation of your personality (individual traits) and couple interaction skills (couple traits) that you take with you as assets or liabilities into marriage. The stronger the base of your Marriage Triangle (that is, family influences), the better prepared you are for marriage. Fortunately, weaknesses resulting from problems in this base can be repaired! In this book you will assess your own base and learn ways to overcome weaknesses traced back to this base.

& Individual Traits

The second major factor in predicting success in marriage is your *individual traits,* including your personality, attitudes, and skills. The specific subfactors that make up this factor include the following:

Traits That Predict Marital Dissatisfaction
- Difficulty coping with stress
- Dysfunctional beliefs
- Excessive:
  Impulsiveness
  Anger and hostility

Depression
Irritability
Anxiety
Self-consciousness

Traits That Predict Marital Satisfaction

- Extroversion

- Flexibility

- Good self-esteem

- Good interpersonal skills (such as assertiveness)

These include personality characteristics related to marital dysfunction (for example, impulsivity) as well as marital satisfaction (for example, flexibility). For an example of how a personality trait can harm marital satisfaction, consider the characteristic of impulsiveness. Impulsive people often act quickly, before thinking. They fail to first consider the consequences of their actions on themselves or others. This may cause marital problems if, for example, the impulsive partner goes out and overspends with a credit card without first considering if the couple can afford the purchases.

In a recent premarital counseling session a young woman complained strongly to me that her fiancé had gone out and charged his VISA card to its maximum level by purchasing appliances and furniture for their new apartment. He reported, "All the stuff was on sale, honey! I just couldn't pass it up!" He had neither discussed the purchases with her before buying these items nor had he first thought about their budget, which was tight just before the wedding. She was rightfully resentful. His impulsivity got both of them into financial trouble!

The role of each personality trait in harming or enhancing your marriage will be described more thoroughly in Chapter Four. I should mention here a generic term, *emotional health*. It is measured mainly by the presence or absence of abnormally high anxiety, depression, and anger. It should be easy to see why marrying a person who is significantly depressed (that is, worse depression than the normal blues we all experience) will lead to problems in marriage—reduced communication, a poor sex life, a lack of positive shared experiences, and so on. You will learn more about these personality traits and their role in marital satisfaction in Chapter Four.

Self-esteem and self-confidence also play a major role in marital satisfaction. People with high self-esteem and self-confidence are more likely to be unselfish, considerate of others, and supportive of others. Low self-esteem leads to the opposite conditions: selfishness, inconsiderateness, and an inability to emotionally support others. You will have the opportunity to evaluate your self-esteem as part of your self-assessment in Chapter Four.

Everyone agrees that marriage is a stressful relationship. No wonder individuals who have difficulty coping with stress report more marital dissatisfaction. The stress of making a living or going to college, paying bills, and maintaining a household require you to learn good stress management skills. You can take positive steps to keep stress from taking over your life—like Joan, who told me, "Before I see Steve after work, I first get relaxed. I learned before marriage that listening to classical music on the way home from work and then drinking a soda and reading the paper before he got home really mellows me. Then I can handle the rest of the evening with Steve."

Dysfunctional beliefs are another component of the individual traits factor. Dysfunctional beliefs we have identified that have a strong negative effect on marital satisfaction include "People cannot change" and "Disagreement in a relationship is bad." Chapter Four discusses in more detail these and other dysfunctional beliefs that can damage your marriage.

Two personality traits that are resources in marriage are extroversion (sometimes referred to as *sociability*) and assertiveness. People who are extroverted and assertive are more likely to have the communication and conflict management skills necessary to form long-term, close personal relationships with others. They are more likely than introverted or nonassertive individuals to be open in their communication with others and understand others' thoughts and feelings. Such relationship maintenance skills are valuable resources later in marriage. As Claudia (twenty-five) said of her boyfriend David (twenty-six): "I'm so glad David is outgoing and open with his feelings. It keeps us from misunderstanding each other. Instead, we can solve problems as they come up. I never wonder what he's thinking or feeling. He tells me!"

 Couple Traits

The third major predictive factor is your *couple traits*. These refer to two important dimensions of your relationship—your communication skills as a couple and certain events or circumstances in your relationship history that predict later marital satisfaction. Perhaps the best way to help you understand the latter point is to give you an example.

Todd (twenty-five) and Tara (nineteen) met at college about six months ago and have recently been discussing if they should get married. The discussion was largely inspired by Tara's discovery that she is pregnant. Todd comes from a wealthy family in Boston; Tara was raised in a poor, blue-collar family in rural Illinois. They express love for each other but are concerned about their very different views on how many children to have, birth control, and the wife's role in marriage. Tara wants to have four children and expects to be a stay-at-home mother, while Todd wants to have two children and expects his wife to work full time and contribute equally to the family finances. The couple have been living together for the last two months as a test "to see if the relationship will work."

How may red lights (that is, danger signs) do you see in this relationship? I count a total of *nine!* In other words, Todd and Tara should be aware of nine danger signs and deal with them before seriously considering marriage. Of these nine red lights, seven are relationship history factors. Here are the nine factors (the relationship factors are marked "RH"):

- Young age at marriage for one or both partners (Tara is nineteen).
- RH: Short length of acquaintance (six months).
- Limited education (both still in college).
- RH: Premarital pregnancy and the resultant pressure to marry.
- RH: Lack of similarity in age.
- RH: Lack of similarity in economic status.
- RH: Lack of similarity in desired number of children and birth control.
- RH: Lack of similarity in expectations for the wife's role.
- RH: Living together as a trial marriage.

In a sense, this marriage is doomed before it begins! If you were Todd or Tara and knew you had nine strikes against you even before you got married, would you still get married? Todd and Tara did. They were divorced thirteen months later.

Other important couple relationship traits that affect later marital satisfaction include premarital sex; degree of similarity of race, intelligence, religion, and overall status; and degree of similarity of values and gender role orientation. I will describe these later, in Chapter Five.

In brief, frequent premarital sexual intercourse with several partners before marriage predicts later marital dissatisfaction, especially for women. Similarity of backgrounds, values, and role orientations in marriage (that is, the wife role and the husband role) predicts marital satisfaction.

The other important dimension of couple traits is the quality of your communication. The better your communication and problem-solving skills, the better your chances for resolving differences and managing your life together. Of all the factors discussed in this book, communication is one of the most important predictors of marital satisfaction. With good communication skills, love, and a kind attitude, many marital conflicts, values differences, and dissimilarities can be resolved successfully.

Communication skills, therefore, are the oil in the engine of marriage. Without them, the engine runs poorly or not at all. Students in my marriage preparation course have commented: "My boyfriend is a great listener. I know after a difficult conversation that he has understood how I feel. That is the basis of solving all of our conflicts!" "The speaking skills I have learned in this course are especially helpful to my fiancé and me. Before learning them, I had no idea why he was so frustrated with me when I would go off on him. Now I can more calmly state my feelings, thoughts, and needs so he is less confused and overwhelmed." More details on assessing communication and problem-solving skills in your relationship are presented in Chapter Five.

Here are the three major factors in the Marriage Triangle model of prediction, along with the more specific subfactors in each area:

Personal and Relationship Contexts	Individual Traits	Couple Traits
	Personality traits	Acquaintanceship
Personal context:	Emotional health	Similarity of values, goals, and expectations
Family-of-origin traits	Self-esteem	
Parent-child relationship	Attitudes and beliefs	Premarital sex and pregnancy
Parents' marital quality	Interpersonal skills	Cohabitation

Personal and Relationship Contexts	Individual Traits	Couple Traits
Age, education, and economic status at marriage		Couple communication and conflict resolution skills

Relationship context:

Parental approval of marriage

Friends' approval of marriage

Internal and external pressures to marry

An example of how these factors work together to predict marital satisfaction or dissatisfaction will be helpful. Ann grew up in a dysfunctional family in which there was high conflict and low cohesion or unity. She seldom felt loved or accepted by her parents (personal context factors at the base of the Marriage Triangle). Thus her self-esteem suffered throughout her life and she was often depressed (individual traits). These factors negatively influenced her decision of both *whom* to marry—she married a man who had very different values but gave her the attention she had always craved—and *when* to marry—she married hurriedly after knowing him for only two months (couple trait), without parental approval (relationship context), at age eighteen (personal context), in an attempt to escape from her cold, rejecting family and finally feel accepted. Ann and her husband were divorced three years later.

Each of the subfactors mentioned here—and its potential influence on your later marital satisfaction—will be described in the remainder of this book, and you will have the opportunity to assess yourself, your relationship, and your contexts to determine how each one may influence your later marital satisfaction.

The first impression you may have after reviewing this list is that predicting marital satisfaction before you marry is more complicated than you originally thought! The purpose of this book is to uncomplicate prediction and help you assess your *marital aptitude*—that is, your readiness to marry as measured by individual, couple, and context assets.

Be assured that you and your partner do *not* have to be perfect in order to keep the odds of a successful marriage in your favor. No matter what, marriage is a risk, for all couples. This book will help you lower your risk of dissatisfaction and divorce and increase your chances of satisfaction and stability. You will do this first by learning about the factors that predict successful marriage; second, by assessing the strengths and weaknesses of yourself, your relationship, and the contexts in which you live; third, by engaging in self- and couple-improvement activities to better prepare yourself for marriage; and fourth, by making a more informed and rational decision about whom to marry and when to marry.

Assessment and the Marriage Triangle

The assessments in this book are called short tests or measures (usually three or four items) of an important factor in the triangle. For example, the assessment of your self-esteem consists of three items that can be answered in about ten seconds. Directions for scoring each short test are included at the end of each chapter. Norm scores (the national average) are usually provided so you can compare your scores to those of thousands of other young adults (aged seventeen to thirty) who have completed the short tests. These comparisons give you an idea of your assets and liabilities. Most norm scores come from a data bank consisting of over five thousand individuals who have taken RELATE over the last three years. Finally, discussion questions based on your results are included at the end of each chapter to help you better understand your assets and liabilities and to help you set goals on how to improve yourself and your relationship.

Guidelines for Using the Assessments

Please note that the assessments are only as valid as you are honest in completing them. Try to be as objective as you can in answering each item. The most important part of the assessment process is discussing what the results mean to you and your partner. Take time to enjoy and take pleasure in your high scores—these scores identify some of the strengths in yourself or your relationship. Look at the areas where you have low scores and discuss their implications.

Some short tests ask you to rate the degree of unity you and your partner have in several important areas (for example, money, working women, birth control, and so on). On these short tests you may find that your unity (agreement) scores are rather low. Your first reaction may be to ignore or deny the differences. Instead, you should meet this challenge head-on. To help you do this, here are some suggestions about how to discuss these issues.[1]

First, look at the differences honestly and openly. It is usually better to face your differences than to deny them or try to avoid them. Find some time when you can discuss your differences in a long, uninterrupted session. Try to determine what is really going on in that aspect of your relationship. This process requires the application of communication and problem-solving skills in a loving environment to iron out the differences in an appropriate manner. Therefore, allow some time to do it; be patient and be a good listener, and try to empathize with your partner's perceptions, too.

Second, remember that some of the short-test results you may need to discuss with your partner are sensitive (for example, family background) and may affect your feelings of self-worth. Ask your partner to be supportive and considerate as you discuss these results. If you become threatened, slow down or even stop and deal with the feelings that are occurring.

Since prediction always contains a certain amount of error, I will not give you direct advice such as, "Marry this person!" or "Don't marry this person!" Instead, the assessments will help you draw your own conclusions about the best course of action for you and your partner.

In summary, you will evaluate the Marriage Triangle as you read this book. The triangle corresponds to three levels of a relationship (see Figure 2.2). As described earlier, each level has its own set of influences. Unfortunately, social scientists do not agree yet on which factor in the triangle best explains why some couples remain happily married while others do not. The most important thing is to be complete in your assessment of these three levels before you marry.

Finally, this book and the assessments herein are limited to premarital factors only. We cannot predict what stressors (for example, chronic fatigue) or crises (for example, accidents) may affect your marriage after the wedding day. A couple may evaluate themselves and their relationship using this book and determine they are a good match, have good mental health and communication skills, and have the support of everyone in their community for their marriage—but still fail ultimately to achieve marital satisfaction. This may occur because marriage is a developing relationship over time. However, starting off on the right foot as emphasized in this book will lessen the chances of your marriage's eventually failing, regardless of the stressors and crises that come your way.

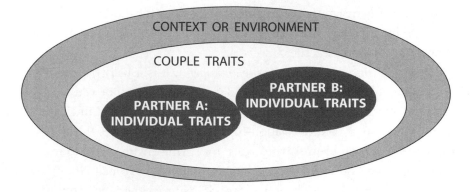

Figure 2.2. Three Levels of a Relationship

As one wife told me about her marriage, "I'm sure glad we were both emotionally healthy and had good self-esteem before we married. That helped us cope with the problems that came into our relationship. Our similarities have helped us to more easily enjoy our lives together. Without good communication skills, we would never have been able to raise our children and solve the day-to-day hassles and decisions that are involved in raising them. It seems like we came into our marriage with most of the necessary tools to make it work!"

Using the Rest of This Book

The next three chapters give more detailed descriptions of the three factors in the marriage triangle and self-assessments on each set of factors. For example, after reading about how self-esteem and personality affect marriage, you will assess your level of self-esteem and several personality characteristics. You will then answer a series of questions about your results and be asked to discuss some of them with your partner.

By the end of these assessments and discussions you will have completed a thorough and meaningful set of assessment exercises that will serve to answer such questions as these:

- How ready am I to get married?

- How ready are we as a couple to get married? (For seriously dating, cohabiting, and engaged couples only.)

- What are the individual and couple assets that will serve as enhancers in a marriage?
- What are the individual and couple liabilities that will limit our chances of a successful marriage?
- What are our individual and couple goals for the future as we prepare for marriage?
- Where can we get more self- and couple-improvement assistance in preparing for marriage? For overcoming personal problems? Couple problems?

The Marriage Triangle, Factor 1

Your Personal and Relationship Contexts

Glenda (twenty-two) became very angry and resentful toward her boyfriend, Pete (twenty-five), whenever he questioned her about problems she was having at work. These same feelings seemed to arise in similar situations whenever someone appeared not to accept her, because she was reminded of her father, who had never accepted her while she was growing up.

Pete had parents with a very conflictual marriage. As a result, he became very anxious every time Glenda brought up the subject of marriage. Several previous relationships had become serious, close to the point of marriage. Each time, Pete broke things off suddenly.

Glenda and Pete experienced these and similar problems in their premarital relationship as a result of their unresolved family-of-origin issues. Your family of origin is the family in which you grew up. When emotionally significant negative interactions or problem relations occur in families (for example, lack of acceptance by a parent or chronic marital conflict) and are not psychologically resolved through healthy discussions with family members, we say that a person has an "unresolved family-of-origin issue" or conflict. These old conflicts keep repeating themselves over and over because people tend to project these internal conflicts into what is happening now. They are "stuck in time"—reliving old situations while dealing with new ones.

In reality, Glenda was not angry at Pete. His questioning was an attempt to better understand her, but it triggered her memories of critical, abusive questioning by her father when she was a teenager and feelings of a lack of acceptance or validation by him. Her anger was really directed at her father, not her boyfriend. She was stuck in time. But Pete felt the negative effects, nonetheless.

To others, Pete rationalized his anxiety about getting married as being the result of feeling unable to support a wife while he was still in college. In reality, his parents' highly conflictual and bitter marriage served as a poor role model for him. Watching their fights caused him great anxiety and despair. As a result of observing their marital conflict, he came to believe that marriage was at best a difficult and frustrating relationship, and he worried that he would have as bad a marriage as his parents did. Hence, he became anxious and depressed whenever a girlfriend hinted that she was interested in marriage. He, too, was stuck in time.

One of the major purposes of this chapter is to help you understand the family-of-origin influences that research suggests have a major impact on your attitudes and feelings about marriage and your later marital satisfaction. Family-of-origin influences, remember, are part of the first dimensions of the Marriage Triangle, personal and relationship contexts.

The first part of this chapter discusses family-of-origin influences. In this section I'll answer the following important questions:

- How does your relationship with your parents when you were growing up affect your later marital satisfaction?

- How will your parents' marriage affect your own marriage?

- Does divorce run in families? Why? How will it affect your marriage?

In the second section I'll answer questions such as these:

- How does your age at marriage affect your later marital satisfaction?

- How does your education level when you marry affect later marital satisfaction?

Last, I will describe the importance of certain relationship contexts in predicting the future success of your marriage and will answer questions such as these:

- Why is it important to get your parents' and friends' approval of your marriage before you marry?
- How can external pressure from others or your own internal pressure force you into a marriage that you should not pursue?

Before I answer these questions, first assess your own individual and relationship contexts by completing and scoring the short tests in Exhibit 3.1.

At the end of the chapter I'll show you how to use the scores and responses in Exhibit 3.1 to determine your strengths and areas for improvement from your background and current situation. But first let's look at the relationship between these contexts and your later marital satisfaction.

🎱 Family-of-Origin Influences

In our longitudinal research with the RELATE we found a positive relationship between healthy family functioning and an individual's later marital satisfaction. Certain kinds of family relationship experiences will either hinder or enhance your later marital satisfaction. These are the family factors most likely to enhance your chances of being happily married:

- Your parents' marriage was a happy one. Their marriage is a role model for what marriage is all about.
- Your relationship with your parents was satisfying, affectionate, and emotionally close. This leads to positive self-esteem, confidence about relationships, trusting others, a desire to become intimate and emotionally close with others, and the ability to make long-term commitments in relationships.
- As an adult, you feel a healthy sense of independence from your parents. For example, you do not feel as if they are trying to run your life or involve you in trying to solve their problems for them. In other words, are you emotionally connected to your parents but not *enmeshed* (too close to them) or *disengaged*

	Strongly Disagree	Disagree	Undecided	Agree	Strongly Agree

Overall Evaluation of Family Processes

1. From what I experienced in my family of origin I think family relationships are safe, secure, rewarding, worth being in, and a source of comfort.

| | 1 | 2 | 3 | 4 | 5 |

2. From what I experienced in my family, I think family relationships are confusing, unfair, anxiety-provoking, inconsistent, and unpredictable.

| | 1 | 2 | 3 | 4 | 5 |

3. We had a loving atmosphere in our family.

| | 1 | 2 | 3 | 4 | 5 |

4. All things considered, my childhood years were happy.

| | 1 | 2 | 3 | 4 | 5 |

First, reverse-score item 2. For example, if you circled 1, score it as 5; score 2 as 4; 3 remains the same. Then sum items 1–4 and write your score here: _____

Parents' Marriage

5. My father was happy in his marriage.

| | 1 | 2 | 3 | 4 | 5 |

6. My mother was happy in her marriage.

| | 1 | 2 | 3 | 4 | 5 |

7. I would like my marriage to be like my parents' marriage.

| | 1 | 2 | 3 | 4 | 5 |

Sum items 5–7 and write your score here: _____

Father-Child Relationships

8. My father showed physical affection to me by appropriate hugging and/or kissing.

| | 1 | 2 | 3 | 4 | 5 |

9. My father participated in enjoyable activities with me.

| | 1 | 2 | 3 | 4 | 5 |

Exhibit 3.1. Assessing Family-of-Origin Issues

	Strongly Disagree	Disagree	Undecided	Agree	Strongly Agree
10. My father and I were able to share our feelings on just about any topic without embarrassment or fear of hurt feelings.	1	2	3	4	5

Sum items 8–10 and write your score here: _____

Mother-Child Relationships

	Strongly Disagree	Disagree	Undecided	Agree	Strongly Agree
11. My mother showed physical affection to me by appropriate hugging and/or kissing.	1	2	3	4	5
12. My mother participated in enjoyable activities with me.	1	2	3	4	5
13. My mother and I were able to share our feelings on just about any topic without embarrassment or fear of hurt feelings.	1	2	3	4	5

Sum items 11–13 and write your score here: _____

Current Impact of Family on You and Your Relationships

	Strongly Disagree	Disagree	Undecided	Agree	Strongly Agree
14. There are matters from my family experience that I'm still having trouble dealing with and coming to terms with.	1	2	3	4	5
15. There are matters from my family experience that negatively affect my ability to form close relationships.	1	2	3	4	5
16. I feel at peace about anything negative that happened to me in the family I grew up in.	1	2	3	4	5

First reverse-score items 14 and 15. Then sum items 14–16 and write your score here:

   _____

Exhibit 3.1. *Continued*

	Strongly Disagree	Disagree	Undecided	Agree	Strongly Agree
				Circle your responses:	

My Independence from Family of Origin

	Strongly Disagree	Disagree	Undecided	Agree	Strongly Agree
17. My parents currently encourage me to be independent and make my own decisions.	1	2	3	4	5
18. My parents currently try to run my life.	1	2	3	4	5

First, reverse-score item 18. Then, sum items 17–18 and write your score here: _____

Parental Conflict Management Style

19. The following is a description of how some parents handle conflict in marriage:

My parents argued often and hotly. There were a lot of insults back and forth, name-calling, put-downs, and sarcasm. They didn't really listen to what the other was saying, nor did they look at each other very much. One or the other of them could be quite detached and emotionally uninvolved, even though there may have been brief episodes of attack and defensiveness. There were clearly more negatives than positives in their relationship.

How often did your parents use this style? (Circle one.)

1. Never

2. Rarely

3. Sometimes

4. Often

5. Very often

Impact of Abuse

20. Sometimes in families conflicts can lead to physical acts that are violent. These acts may include slapping, pushing, kicking, hitting hard with a fist, hitting with objects, or other types of violence.

Exhibit 3.1. *Continued*

Considering all of your experiences while growing up in your family, how would you rate the general level of violence in your home? (Circle your response.)

1. There was never violence in the home.

2. There was rarely violence in the home.

3. There was sometimes violence in the home.

4. There was often violence in the home.

5. There was very often violence in the home.

21. Sometimes in families sexual activities occur that are inappropriate. These acts may include a parent or sibling fondling a child, a parent or sibling engaging in sexual intercourse with a child, or some other type of inappropriate sexual activity.

   Considering all of your experiences while growing up in your family, how often did one or more of these inappropriate sexual activities happen to you? (Circle your response.)

   1. Never

   2. Rarely

   3. Sometimes

   4. Often

   5. Very often

22. How often was someone outside your family (not your current partner) sexually abusive toward you? (Circle your response.)

   1. Never

   2. Rarely

   3. Sometimes

   4. Often

   5. Very Often

Exhibit 3.1. *Continued*

Parental Mental Health

23. In your immediate family while you grew up, how often did your parent or parents experience emotional problems such as serious depression, anxiety attacks, eating disorders, alcohol or drug abuse, or other mental or emotional problems? (Circle your response.)

   1. Never

   2. Rarely

   3. Sometimes

   4. Often

   5. Very often

Family Status

24. Circle the type of family situation in which you spent the most time while growing up (to age eighteen):

   1. One parent because of divorce.

   2. One parent because of death.

   3. Both biological parents.

   4. A parent and a stepparent.

   5. A foster family.

   6. An adoptive family.

   7. A relative (for example, grandparent).

Personal Characteristics

25. How old do you project that you will be when you get married? (Fill in blank.) _____

26. How old will your partner be? (Fill in blank.) _____

27. What will be your estimated couple yearly gross income when you get married? (Fill in blank.) _____

28. What will be your estimated total couple debt when you get married? (Fill in blank.) _____

Exhibit 3.1. *Continued*

29. Estimate how many years of education after high school you will have completed when you get married. (Fill in blank.) _____

30. Estimate how many years of education after high school your partner will have completed when you get married. (Fill in blank.) _____

Parents' and Friends' Approval

The next group of items concerns you and your current partner. If you are not seriously dating, engaged, or living together, you should still read each item, but may leave your answers blank.

How much do the following individuals approve of your current relationship:

Circle your responses:

	Not at all	Somewhat	Mostly	Entirely	Don't know
31. Your father	1	2	3	4	5
32. Your mother	1	2	3	4	5
33. Your friends	1	2	3	4	5
34. Your partner's father	1	2	3	4	5
35. Your partner's mother	1	2	3	4	5
36. Your partner's friends	1	2	3	4	5

Internal and External Pressures

37. In your current relationship, who is moving faster toward marriage? (Circle your answer.)

   1. I want to get married much more than my partner.

   2. I want to get married a little more than my partner.

   3. My partner wants to get married a little more than I do.

   4. My partner wants to get married much more than I do.

   5. We are both moving fast.

Exhibit 3.1. *Continued*

6. Neither of us is moving fast.

7. Does not apply.

38. How much pressure to get married from others or yourself do you feel right now? (Circle your answer.)

1. No pressure

2. Some pressure

3. Much pressure

Exhibit 3.1. *Continued*

(too distant from them) emotionally? Emotional independence frees you to pursue intimate relations with your peers. It is a healthy stage of personality development.

- Your family communication is open and honest without being hurtful. Thus you have learned how to express yourself appropriately, listen well, and resolve conflicts in a healthy way.

By contrast, these family factors are the ones most likely to inhibit your chances of being happily married:

- Your parents' marriage was an unhappy one.
- Your parents got a divorce.
- Your relationship with your parents was unsatisfying, emotionally cold, detached, neglectful, or abusive.
- Your parents are emotionally enmeshed or overinvolved in your life, controlling or intimidating you, or overly dependent on you.
- You observed chronic hostile marital conflict between your parents while you were growing up.

Perhaps an example of these latter family dynamics will be useful here.

The Enmeshed Son Story

When I was doing marriage counseling in a university counseling center, I once saw a young couple whose major complaint after a year of marriage involved the husband's family-of-origin problems, which had started long before their wedding.

The problem was this: The husband's parents had an unsatisfying, conflictual marriage. The problem was chronic—it had lasted for more than twenty years, yet they were still married. When the arguments got too hot, my client's mother would call her son and ask him to come over for a meal or some other social gathering. While at the meal or gathering, both parents would pull my client aside and take turns complaining about each other, each parent trying to convince him to side with them. His mother divulged to him that he had always "helped keep their marriage together" and "she didn't know what she would do" without his help. This led him to feel depressed when his mother felt so bad. Their emotional lives were enmeshed.

Needless to say, these visits to his family of origin caused a great deal of anxiety for him and his wife. His wife went with him on these occasions, but he virtually ignored her while he was doing his amateur counseling. He would return home after a visit angry and frustrated at his parents and she would return hurt and resentful that her husband ignored her and let himself get caught up in a problem his parents should solve on their own.

It was easy to see that this newly married husband was trying to serve as a marriage counselor for his parents. This role kept him from separating from his family and accepting a job that he wanted to take in another state—despite his wife's enthusiastic support for the prospective change. He felt guilty and anxious even thinking about leaving his parents to solve their problems on their own.

This couple came to my office because of the tension and disruption the enmeshment with his family of origin caused them as a couple. The wife demanded that he cut off this unhealthy relationship with his family. But he felt too guilty and anxious about his parents' marriage and his role in resolving their problems to act appropriately by setting firmer boundaries.

The husband was a bit shocked when I suggested that he turn over his marriage counseling role to a licensed professional, but ultimately a great sense of relief came to both their faces when he agreed! Getting himself out of this dysfunctional, enmeshed family-of-origin problem gave him more emotional strength and time to develop his role as a husband in his young marriage.

Research has identified several other family dynamics that will hinder your chances of having a satisfactory marriage. They are parental mental illness, hostile parental conflict styles, child neglect or abuse, and parental marital dissatisfaction or divorce.

Parental Mental Illness

If one or both of your parents had a mental health problem (clinical depression, phobia, chronic anxiety, addiction, or some other condition) it probably strained their marriage and hindered their parenting. A parent with a serious mental health problem usually has trouble expressing affection to other family members, providing love, and building self-esteem in his or her children. The child then grows up feeling insecure and unloved—feelings that negatively affect dating and eventual marriage.

This happened to a woman I counseled during my first internship as a doctoral student. She was experiencing conflict with her husband because of her low self-esteem. It seemed that he could not ever do enough for her to convince her she was OK. She related that while she was growing up her mother suffered from untreated clinical depression and rarely performed her duties as a wife or mother. She was too tired, depressed, and irritable to speak kindly to her daughter, my client. She rarely said anything to her that was esteem building. She failed to attend my client's recitals, parent-teacher conferences, or soccer games. My client grew up thinking her mother hated her and—as children do—she came to believe she was worthy of hate. This self-hate was polluting her marriage now and making it difficult for her to bond to her husband. She even stated in a counseling session, "I still don't see what he sees in me that keeps him around!"

Hostile Parental Conflict Management

The conflict management styles learned from your parents will transfer into your own marriage. After all, your parents served as your role models for conflict resolution. One style that hinders effective conflict management in marriage is a hostile, attacking and defending style with a goal to hurt the other. Another style that seldom works is complete avoidance of conflict or disagreements. In this style, spouses simply refuse to deal with their issues openly, often because they are afraid they cannot solve them or are afraid of conflict. Frustration, anger, and resentment are often the results of unresolved conflict.

Marital researcher John Gottman has found that happily married couples may resolve conflict in one of three different ways.[1] Each way seems to work and contributes to marital satisfaction. The first type is called *volatile*. Volatile couples engage in discussions in an enthusiastic manner. They do not try to understand or empathize with each other, but rather, each spouse tries to persuade the other. For them, "winning is what it's all about." Their conflicts are volcanic but just a small part of an otherwise warm and loving marriage.

Type two conflict is called the *avoidant* style.[2] Conflict avoiders minimize their differences rather than resolving them. They neither attempt to persuade nor to compromise; very little gets settled. They "agree to disagree." They make light of their differences. However, this pattern does *not* lead to marital dissatisfaction. Rather than resolve conflicts, these couples "appeal to their basic shared philosophy of marriage." They love each other, accentuate the positives, and accept their differences. This style is different from the avoidant style mentioned earlier, where spouses do not even *try* to resolve differences. In that case, there is no discussion of problems—total avoidance—because of a lack of communications skills, conflict phobia, or chronic discouragement from never solving their conflicts.

The third successful style is called the *validating* style.[3] This is the style that marriage counselors think is the ideal. We try to teach couples this style in counseling and marriage enrichment workshops. Validators listen to each other respectfully and after both partners feel they have fully aired their opinions, they each attempt to gain the other's agreement. "Attempts to convince each other are good natured with no arm-twisting." Many times they resolve conflicts with compromise.

The last type of conflict resolution described by Gottman is characteristic of unhappily married couples and is referred to as *hostile*. Couples who use this style insult each other. Neither person listens. The arguments usually end in hurt feelings and resentfulness. This conflict resolution pattern predicts divorce for most couples!

Child Abuse or Neglect

The most serious family-of-origin influences include child neglect, abuse, or parental alcohol or drug dependency. Neglect and abuse damage a person's self-esteem and may lead to chronic depression, anxiety, and resentment toward parents, or more serious mental health problems that can poison a marriage. Parental alcohol or drug dependency damages the parent's ability to provide a stable, predictable, and healthy parent-child relationship and a satisfying marriage. The results of the damage to the psychological or interpersonal functioning of offspring of alcoholics is seen in the higher divorce rate of adult children of alcoholics compared to adult children of nonalcoholics. And many of these adult children become alcoholics themselves. Later in this chapter I discuss how to overcome the effects of these kinds of dysfunctional family patterns on you and your later marital adjustment.

Here is another example of the effects of child abuse on one's later marital satisfaction. A couple in their late twenties came to me for help with the problem of chronic conflict over when to have children, how many children to have, and how to raise them. They currently had one three-year-old son. Both the husband and the wife traced the conflict between them back to the wife's experience with emotional abuse by her mother. During most of the wife's life, her mother told her she was ugly and fat, and that no "normal boy" would ever want her. Her mother even listened to her telephone calls to boyfriends and teased her about them. Earlier in life, she had also physically abused this daughter.

In therapy, the wife explained to me, "I learned as a child that children are to be despised, never wanted. I never felt wanted. So why would *I* want another child? Why would *anyone* want to be a parent? I guess my husband will just have to raise our three-year-old. I can't!"

This is a tragic story because this young mother was failing to bond with her son. An absence of healthy mother-child bonding can lead to serious psychological problems for children. The father felt inadequate to provide enough emotional support for his son to make up the difference. He threatened to divorce his wife if she did not deal with her issues from the past and better mother their son. As a result, she entered therapy, which eventually led to her reconciling with her mother and forgiving her for the past. Not all stories of the effects of childhood abuse in adulthood are this bad; yet some are even worse. The point is that abuse frequently traumatizes a person to the point that without therapy they will have a higher than average chance of having marital difficulties.

It is a tribute to the resilience of the human spirit that some neglect and abuse victims suffer few psychological problems or later marital problems even without professional therapy. Social scientists are just beginning to understand the resiliency or hardiness some individuals exhibit.

The Effects of Your Parents' Marriage

Several factors from your parents' marriage may have major influences on your marriage: Their degree of marital satisfaction, the amount of hostile marital conflict, and divorce. Your exposure to chronic hostile marital conflict will probably make you anxious and depressed. Children who experience such conflict are also exposed to poor role models for handling marital disagreements and are less likely to learn good communication and conflict-resolution skills that they can use in their own marriage.

Here are some of the lessons you may take from being exposed to hostile marital conflict:

- Relationships are frightening and unpredictable.
- Relationships are dangerous.
- Relationships bring sadness, resentment, and hurt.
- Disagreement is bad because it always results in hurt feelings.
- Marriage is where you fight.

Perhaps your parents did not fight often but still were very dissatisfied. Such chronic marital dissatisfaction may have taught you these lessons:

- Marriage is painful.
- Fulfillment is not found in relationships.
- Long suffering—that's marriage!
- Putting up with one another is what marriage is all about.
- People get stuck in marriage.

Such lessons may be difficult to erase from your mind and could ultimately lessen your chances of marital satisfaction by creating a negative mind-set about marriage.

The Impact of Divorce

There is considerable evidence that divorce seems to "run in families"—that is, persons whose parents divorced are somewhat more likely to divorce than persons whose parents had stable marriages.[4] Why? Although many explanations for this phenomenon have been offered, only a few have research support.

First, it appears that offspring of families of divorce have a greater willingness to resort to divorce as a solution to marital problems than people from intact families. It is as if their parents' divorce served as a role model for divorce. They also may be said to have a lower commitment to marriage, thinking, "If my parents' marriage failed, mine can, too. Since marriage is so fragile, I'd better not put all my eggs in one basket," or, "Like my dad, I'll give this marriage a good shot. If it doesn't work out, I have the option of getting out." Divorce, then, is more plausible to many children of divorce than to children of intact marriages. They saw their parents divorce and survive it all. Thus, on the average, they may more likely to resort to divorce when serious marriage problems arise.

Second, children of divorce tend to marry at a younger age than persons from intact families. For some children of divorce, early marriage offers an escape from an unpleasant family situation or it fills an emotional need created by the trauma of parental divorce. It is well-known that persons who marry at a relatively young age (roughly under twenty) are more likely to divorce.[5]

Third, recent research suggests that offspring of divorced parents compared to those from intact families may more likely develop interpersonal behaviors that harm marital satisfaction. These include problems with anger, jealousy, hurt feelings, trust, communication, or infidelity. These problems are related both to poor parental marital quality and to divorce of parents. Such problematic interpersonal behaviors increase your risk of divorce.

These traits were exhibited in Carrie (twenty-one), a young woman I met while I working at a university counseling center. She came to therapy to get help with her "low self-esteem," which kept leading to problems with boyfriends. She had just broken up with her latest one. She wanted to know what she was contributing to these relationship failures. Her family history showed that she grew up in a family where her parents divorced when she was sixteen. The divorce was the result of her father's having been caught in an affair by her mother. This revelation devastated both Carrie and her mother. Even five years later she was still resentful toward her father for "breaking up our family."

We investigated how she related to boyfriends in the here-and-now. She emphasized that all of them eventually became tired of her "unrelenting jealousy and possessiveness" and mistrust of them. Her insecurity in these relationships was related to her relationship with her father and his cheating on her mother. She was easily hurt and would respond with anger, which was unconsciously directed toward her father, not her partner of the moment. It took her just a few sessions of therapy to gain these insights. Then we worked on ridding her of these insecurities, negative feelings, and extreme behaviors. Her relationships with boyfriends, as a result, improved greatly.

Another example of the effects of parental divorce on offspring is Julie and

Richard, a couple I saw in premarital counseling at the prompting of his mother. In fact, his mother demanded that they receive counseling if they expected her to come to the wedding! She contacted me before the couple came and explained her concern that her son learned many bad habits from observing her marriage and divorce. She described her former relationship with his father as emotionally distant and unfulfilling. They lived the last ten years of their marriage like roommates. They rarely spoke to each other except to conduct family or financial business. She divorced him after first engaging in two extramarital affairs. She was currently remarried to a man with whom she had a more intimate and meaningful relationship.

Her chief concern was that her son would be emotionally unavailable to his wife. She said, "Richard's father was a poor role model for a husband. And I nagged his father endlessly for attention and love but got neither. I don't want this to happen to Julie! I want Richard to understand what a really intimate relationship is like—full of sharing, affection, self-disclosure, and all that. Can you teach him that?"

I told her it would take time and experience, but that I would assess Richard's ability to be intimate with Julie as a part of the premarital counseling. I found that he, like his father, seldom showed his thoughts, feelings, or needs. In private he said to me, "Women cannot be trusted with your innermost feelings" and "Never turn your back 'cause she may leave you for another guy!" Julie reported that he often "put up a wall" between them and she felt shut out of his life. She naively reassured me that he would be "an open book" after they got married. I countered with my twenty years of clinical experience and warned her that that was very unlikely. I spent four months helping Richard with his trust issues, the hurt feelings caused by his mother's infidelity and divorce, and his problem identifying and describing his feelings in words—a trait that he learned from his father and other stoic men in his extended family. Richard improved a lot and Julie was more fulfilled in the relationship. Richard's mother, too, was relieved that the effort may have prevented the intergenerational transmission of divorce in her family.

Overcoming the Negative Effects of Divorce

Lest this divorce discussion discourage you if you are a child of divorce, let me offer some reassuring comments. First, if you exhibit such problematic behaviors, or "emotional allergies," the relationship may still survive or even thrive if your partner has good communication skills, is trusting, and is highly committed to the relationship.[6] Second, if you are already aware of these problems (for example, a problem trusting your prospective mate), you can learn how to be more trusting and act in more appropriate ways through professional therapy before marriage.

In addition, you should not interpret this discussion to mean that divorce is inevitable for the children of divorce or that persons from divorced families should never marry. These are the crucial questions you must ask if you or your partner come from a divorced family: How did your parents' marital dissatisfaction and divorce affect you emotionally at the time it occurred? How do you feel about it now? How did your parents' marital dissatisfaction and divorce affect your development of communication and problem-solving skills? What are your attitudes about commitment in marriage? About divorce? How did your parents' divorce affect these attitudes? What unresolved feelings or problems with trust, jealousy, anger, and so on do you need to deal with related to their divorce? (Write here:)

_____

_____

_____

_____

_____

_____

It is interesting to note that in some cases parental divorce serves as a positive experience for children affected by it. It may motivate them to develop better communication skills, or to commit more fully to marriage than their parents did. This attitude was reflected in a statement my first college roommate made to me one day. We were discussing our family backgrounds and he noted that his parents had divorced when he was only nine years old. He said it really hurt him. Then he said to me, "I'll never let that happen to me! I'm not getting married until I'm sure it will work. I'm going to be real careful." I noticed that he did not date at all his freshman year in college. Although not dating at all when you're eighteen is rare in our society, many parents like me wish their kids would wait until then or later to start!

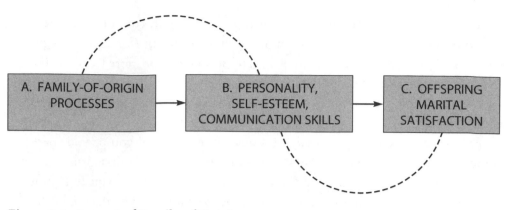

Figure 3.1. Impact of Family of Origin

Indirect Effects of Family of Origin

I said earlier that family-of-origin issues may have a more indirect than direct effect on your later marital satisfaction. Figure 3.1 shows why this effect may be indirect. In research, we seldom find a strong direct relationship (solid arrow) between family-of-origin processes (box A) and the marital satisfaction of offspring (box C).

Rather, we usually find a stronger relationship between family-of-origin processes (for example, family cohesion, abuse, alcoholism) and one's personality and self-esteem (individual traits), and couple communication skills (couple traits). These intermediate factors in turn affect one's marital satisfaction. This shows how the enduring strength and influence of family factors at the base of the Marriage Triangle may affect your later marital satisfaction. The broken line between family-of-origin processes, personality, and so on and marital satisfaction represents this indirect but nonetheless important relationship between box A and box C. The relationship is said to be indirect because the factors in box A affect box C through box B. What family-of-origin processes described in this chapter have affected your personality, self-esteem, and couple communication skills? How will these effects increase or decrease your future marital satisfaction? (Write here:)

_____

_____

_____

_____

_____

_____

📟 Personal Context

In addition to your family background, several other personal characteristics at the time of your marriage will influence your later marital satisfaction. They are important assets or liabilities you bring to your marriage on your wedding day. One group of factors includes your age, education, income level, occupational status, and employment status at marriage.[7] These five factors are obviously closely related to each other—for example, younger individuals are less likely than older individuals to be employed full time, have a college education, have an adequate income for marriage, and have high occupational status (for example, a medical doctor has a higher occupational status than a truck driver).

Most important, younger individuals are usually less emotionally and financially mature than older individuals. They are less likely to have real-life independent living experiences including taking care of themselves financially, cooking, housekeeping, paying bills, coping with new surroundings, making new friends, learning how to live successfully with others (that is, roommates), solving daily problems without the assistance of parents, and so on. The advantages of living independently away from one's family of origin are, thus, enormous! In addition, the older you are at marriage, the more dating experience you will usually have, too. An abundance of dating experiences helps a person better determine the type of person they want to marry and gives them a chance to compare partners on a variety of important personal characteristics.

Finally, a word about marrying when under age twenty—_do not do it!_ The divorce rate is nearly twice as high for those who do.[8] A professional demographer and colleague of mine, Dr. Tim Heaton, recently completed research on marital stability that shows that the chances of divorce for a woman go down to their lowest level if she is twenty-three or older at marriage.[9] That makes sense if you consider that for many women the five years after high school give them time to complete college and one year of work experience or graduate school before marriage. Sounds good to me!

In summary, the following are related to marital dissatisfaction and divorce, and hence are liabilities you may bring to your marriage:

- Young age (especially if under age twenty).
- Limited education (especially the lack of a high school education).
- Relatively low income.
- Low occupational status (that is, having an occupation that is not respected by society, or—more important—by your future spouse).
- Unemployment. (Who can afford to get married if they are unemployed?)

What does this mean for you in terms of *when* to get married? My advice is simple: Make these five factors assets for your marriage:

- *Get married at a relatively older age* (roughly, mid-twenties or later).
- *Complete as much education as possible before you marry.* This is true for women as well as men. Tim Heaton notes that in addition to older age as a resource for marriage, a woman's education can have a positive impact. "A woman's improved educational status provides her with the tools to promote equality within the relationship and enhance her marriage."
- *Marry when your income is relatively high.* Since "high" is a vague term, I define it as enough to support the two of you at a level you can realistically expect at the beginning of a marriage. For couples still going to college or vocational school, this amount will be less than for those who have graduated and are fully employed.
- *Seek the highest occupational status you can,* given your interests, needs, personality, intelligence, and financial resources.
- *At minimum, have a steady and secure job, with benefits.*

A special caution here! The relationships between education, occupational status, and marital satisfaction should not be interpreted to necessarily mean that couples should wait until they have finished college and have prestigious occupations before they get married! There is no evidence that couples who marry while one or both partners are in college or vocational school have higher divorce rates than those who wait until after graduation to marry. Those still in school just have to cope with what I call "relative poverty" until they get their first good jobs!

❦ Relationship Contexts

When you marry it won't be in a vacuum. You don't just marry a person, you marry a whole family. Thus, your parents' and your partner's parents' opinions and approval of your marriage are important to consider before marrying. Research shows that parental opposition to marriage is related to marital problems and divorce.[10]

Your parents should be viewed as resources in helping you select a spouse. They can give you important (although sometimes biased) feedback about the person you are considering marrying. They serve as a second opinion on the suitability of the match between you and your partner. Their opinion helps you in a number of ways:[11]

- It helps you see compatibilities or incompatibilities that may be blind spots for you. Since your parents know you better than any other adults, their perceptions can be very important and valuable.

- It validates that you are making a good choice of a spouse. This will enhance your confidence in your marriage.

- It increases the chances they will support you and your spouse later, when you need their assistance.

- It lowers the chances of their criticizing your partner or you later.

- It lowers the chances they will isolate you and your partner later because they are preparing for the demise of your relationship.

Friends' approval is important, too, for the same reasons.

What if your parents or friends disapprove of your marriage, but you are strongly in favor of it? What should you do? The key is *balance*—balancing your own feelings and opinions with those of your parents and friends.[12] If their feelings and opinions differ greatly from your own, I suggest the following solutions from Neil Warren's book, *Finding the Love of Your Life*.[13]

1. Keep an open mind—remember, you have the final decision!

2. Take plenty of time to consider the feedback you are receiving from significant others. Get all the relevant information. Compare the opinions of others. Is there consensus? Or, what common concern do all parties have that you should consider?

3. If you and your parents or friends still disagree about your marriage ideas, try getting the opinion of a more objective third party, for example, a clergy person, a professor or teacher, or a professional therapist. Compare these opinions with each other.

4. If you are still troubled, seek professional therapy.

5. Finally, *beware!* If your parents and friends are *certain* about your choice of a spouse but you are not, *do not go forward with the wedding!*

That does not necessarily mean breaking up with your partner. You may want to continue to date and gather more information and observations. Also, remember that sometimes others' opinions of your marriage or partner change after they become better acquainted with your partner. So, go slow—let them get to know your partner better.

Remember, in the final analysis, *it is easier and less painful to break off a relationship before you marry than after!*

Realistic examples of the negative effects of parental disapproval on children's marriages can be seen in two popular movies: *Love Story* and *She's Having a Baby*. Both movies are about a couple falling in love, deciding to marry, and dealing with the first year of marriage.

In *Love Story* (the more serious example), there is strong parental disapproval of the marriage from both sides of the family. The couple—Jenny and Oliver—marry anyway. The negative effects of this disapproval on the marriage are painful to watch. In one scene, the new wife is talking to her husband's father about his upcoming birthday party. Jenny holds out the phone and asks Oliver to talk directly to his father. Oliver refuses because of built-up resentment for his father's disapproving the marriage and putting down Jenny's blue-collar background. This causes Jenny and Oliver to have an explosive argument that results in Jenny's leaving the apartment in tears.

The negative effects of parental disapproval are more humorously illustrated in the black comedy *She's Having a Baby*. The disapproval starts when Kristi brings Jake home to meet her family for the first time and continues unmercifully through the birth of their first child. Each time the couple needs emotional or financial support from their parents, none is given because of their continuing opposition. This puts great stress on the marriage. It also damages both parties' self-esteem. So, depending on the mood you are in, watch one of these movies and discuss the effects of parental disapproval with your partner!

⚅ External and Internal Pressures: What Are They?

Often, influences beyond family and friends may later affect a couple's satisfaction. Research shows that the following circumstances may pressure a couple into getting married when perhaps they should not do so.

Job or Career Circumstances

Some couples decide to get married impulsively just before he leaves for boot camp in the military (this was very popular during World War II) or just before she takes a great job two thousand miles away. In these cases, the couples allow an important event to pressure them into getting married prematurely. They may not know each other well enough yet. Or maybe one of them really wanted to finish college first. Perhaps one of them fears, "If we don't get married now, we never will!"

Don't let these kinds of pressure push you into a premature decision to get married. If it really is true love, it will last, even if your partner is moving ten thousand miles away!

Limited Opportunities

Some people feel pressured to marry the most eligible person in their hometown of five hundred people! In such situations, the pool of eligible partners is necessarily very limited. So they marry someone who is not really a very good match for them, thinking, "You're not much but you've got to be better than no one at all!"

Not true! Such thinking may work when selecting a car, home, or what to eat for dinner. But settling for second best in the most important relationship decision of your life is not wise. If the pool of eligible partners is small where you live, *move to a larger city!* Or, as I frequently tell single young adults anxious to get married, "You must sit close to the fire to get warm!" Don't take second best in marriage!

A personal example of this phenomenon may illustrate this idea. My freshman year at college was frustrating because the pool of eligible women was tiny. I wanted to date women who shared my religion, but at the university I attended (twenty thousand students), I found a total of five single women whom I wanted to date who shared my religious values and were about my age! Perhaps I didn't look long or closely enough to find the right girl; nevertheless, I was frustrated and discouraged. So at the end of the year, I transferred to another university in a different state where my pool of eligible women went up to approximately two thousand single women with my same religious values, all about my age! I thought I had died and gone to heaven! As a result, my GPA went from a 3.50 to a 2.65 in one semester due to all the extracurricular girl-related activities I was engaged in. I never regretted that decision. (I met my future wife at church there, by the way—but it took several enjoyable years of looking, first.)

It took courage and sacrifice on my part to transfer—I gave up a good academic scholarship at the first university in order to transfer. But it was worth it! Remember, *whom you marry is the single most important decision you will ever make!* So don't take it casually or settle for a Chevy when what you really want is a Porsche.

Pressure from Family or Friends

Another source of pressure to marry may come from the people closest to you—parents or friends, or perhaps from a clergy person. When most young adults in the U.S. reach the age of twenty-five or thirty, just about everyone close to them applies some pressure on them to "hurry up and get hitched."

I remember one time being in love with a girl whose mother told her in front of me at a family dinner that she "heard wedding bells ringing!" This was her not-so-subtle way of applying pressure. This daughter was the oldest in a family of five girls and felt the responsibility of marrying first.

The problem here was that *I* did not hear the same wedding bells ringing and I told her that! In fact, her mother's pressure on us actually backfired. I felt very uncomfortable as a result of this comment and similar ones she made that evening.

Although I loved the girl at the time, I did not want to marry her. We broke up shortly after that. One year later I saw her again. She proudly announced that she was engaged. She also made an interesting comment: "I finally found a guy who couldn't say no to me and my mother!" Wow, I think I dodged a bullet! I wonder if she's still married?

Marriage is a choice you should look forward to with joy, excitement, and anticipation—not dread! *Never get married to get people off your back!*

Pressure from Within Yourself

Some people are their own worst enemy when it comes to marrying because they put undue pressure on themselves to marry too soon or to marry an inappropriate person. Reasons for this internal anxiety or pressure include beliefs like these:

"Unless I marry this person now, he or she will *never* marry me!"

"This is the best chance I will ever get, so what the heck?"

"No one else will want me."

"I'm lonely, so I should marry the first person who will pay attention to me."

"I'm getting too old to still be single."

"What will people think of me if I'm thirty-five and still single?"

There are probably another dozen such unrealistic beliefs that create anxiety and pressure to take the plunge either before you should or with an inappropriate person. Of course, an overactive sex drive also results in premature marriages (often in Las Vegas).

If you feel overly anxious because you are still single, the solution is first to become aware of such unrealistic beliefs and then to counter these beliefs with more realistic and healthier ideas. For example, "This is the best chance I will ever get" can be revised to "This looks like a promising relationship, but I need to give it more time so I make a well-informed decision." "I'm getting too old to still be single" can be revised to, "I'm older than I'd like to be and still single, but if I continue to date and make the best of my talents and abilities, marriage will eventually come along." The "What will people think of me . . . " belief is easily modified to, "I cannot control what others think of me, so I'll be satisfied to be the kind of person *I* want to be and make choices that make *me* happy." Changing beliefs may require professional therapy. *Do not get married to relieve your anxiety!* Relieve your anxiety in therapy first.

An Overview of All Contextual Factors

Let's review the factors in your individual and relationship contexts that predict your future marital satisfaction. These context factors will *inhibit* your chances of having a satisfying marriage:

- A poor relationship with your parents during your childhood.
- Chronic parental marital dissatisfaction, conflict, or divorce.
- An unaffectionate, cold, distant family of origin.
- Unhealthy emotional enmeshment with your parents.
- Parents' and friends' disapproval of your marriage.
- Marrying younger than age twenty.
- Little postsecondary education, low occupational status, and low income at marriage.
- Pressure from family, friends, outsiders, or yourself to marry when you are not ready.

Put in a more positive way, you can expect to have more marital satisfaction if you

- Come from a functional family that was warm, accepting, had good communication skills, and fostered healthy independence for you.
- Have happily married parents.
- Have parents' and friends' approval of your marriage.

- Marry after age twenty, and have finished your education, are in a respected occupation, and making an adequate income.
- Feel little pressure from family, friends, or yourself to get married.

Unfortunately, social scientists don't know which of the factors are most important and which are least important. My opinion is that family-of-origin factors, parental marriage, age at marriage, approval, and lack of pressure are most important. The less important factors are education level, occupational status, and income at the time of marriage. Most couples expect to struggle a bit financially at first after marriage—comfort helps as you settle down together, but as long as you're off to a reasonable start you don't need to be on top of the world.

So how do you and your partner measure up on these important background and personal factors? To get a better idea, let's look at your scores on the assessments you completed at the beginning of the chapter.

❧ Evaluating Your Own Test Results

Now, the most exciting part of the chapter! The scoring and interpretation guidelines below are divided into the same three sections as the rest of this chapter, namely:

- Family-of-origin scores and interpretation guidelines
- Personal context scores and interpretation guidelines
- Relationship contexts and interpretation guidelines

Before first looking at your family-of-origin test results, I want to give you a couple of guidelines for interpreting your test scores:

First, if in examining and discussing your results you or your partner feel uncomfortable, confused, or unsure of how to interpret the results, consider taking your results to a clergy person or therapist who does premarital counseling, who can assist you.

Second, put the scores in context. The range of scores on the short tests are listed so you know where your score fits in with the lowest and highest scores possible. The norm score also is listed. Most norm scores refer to the average score received for over five thousand individuals who have completed these short tests from the RELATE instrument over the last two years. By comparing your scores to these national norms, you will better understand how similar or different you are from others.

Now let's look at your scores for the family-of-origin items.

In Exhibit 3.2, write in your sum scores on each short test you completed in Exhibit 3.1. These scores are your assessments of your family-of-origin functioning and influences on you.

Family-of-Origin Factors

Now think about the numbers you see in Exhibit 3.2. First, what are your highest scores? What are your lowest scores? Which scores are at or below the low score levels?

How have your family-of-origin experiences, including your parent-child relationships, affected your self-esteem? Your ability to relate to others? Your ability to trust others? How has your parents' marriage affected you? How has it served as either a poor or good role model for your marriage? What qualities from your parents' marriage do you want to cultivate in your own marriage? What patterns do you want to avoid? Why?

_____

_____

_____

_____

_____

_____

How do these family-of-origin factors affect your attitudes and feelings about marriage? How do they affect your readiness to marry? Why?

_____

_____

Overall Evaluation of Family Process Score (questions 1–4): _____

      Range: 4–20   Norm score: .... 17.2   Low: 14.1

Parents' Marriage Score (questions 5–7): _____

      Range: 3–15   Norm score: .... 11.0   Low: 7.4

Father-Child Relationship Score (questions 8–10): _____

      Range: 3–15   Norm score: .... 10.9   Low: 8.0

Mother-Child Relationship Score (questions 11–13): _____

      Range: 3–15   Norm score: .... 12.1   Low: 9.7

Current Impact of Family Score (questions 14–16): _____

      Range: 3–15   Norm score: .... 11.2   Low: 8.2

Independence from Family Score (questions 17–18): _____

      Range: 2–10   Norm score: .... 8.5   Low: 7.0

Exhibit 3.2. Family-of-Origin Assessment Summary

_____

_____

_____

_____

Victor Cline explains nicely how a positive relationship with an opposite sex parent may help you as a spouse: "If one has had the advantage of a good relationship with a parent of the opposite gender, it can strengthen a person to tolerate a difficult spouse through harried and stressful times. Supported by such happy childhood experiences, a husband or wife is prepared to expect good things. Their unconsciousness tells them, 'Better days are ahead.'"[14]

How much independence do you have in your relationship with your parents? How does this affect your readiness for marriage? Your self-confidence as a future husband or wife? Your ability to leave home to establish a new, separate marital relationship?

_____

_____

_____

_____

_____

Parental Conflict Management Style

Now, examine your answer to item 19 in Exhibit 3.1. This item deals with a hostile way of handling conflict in marriage, which researchers have identified as dysfunctional. If you answered item 19 as "Sometimes," "Often," or "Very Often," answer these questions:

How has your parents' style of conflict management affected you emotionally? What has their style taught you about marriage and how to manage conflict in marriage? How do you currently deal with conflict in close relationships with friends and others?

_____

_____

_____

_____

_____

If your parents did not use the hostile conflict management style as described in item 19, describe how they managed conflict:

_____

_____

_____

_____

_____

What did you learn from your parents about managing conflict? Will you manage conflict in a similar or different manner? Why?

_____

_____

_____

_____

_____

Impact of Abuse

Items 20–22 refer to abuse you may have experienced while growing up. Since the nature of these questions is very personal and sensitive, if you answered *any* of these items with a score of 2 or higher ("Rarely" through "Very Often"), it is important that you discuss your answers to these questions with a trusted friend, dating partner, parent, clergy person, teacher, therapist, or someone else whom you trust. Talk to whomever you feel most comfortable with. However, be aware that if you are under eighteen years old and report child abuse or neglect to any adult, they are *required by law* in most states to report the incident to legal authorities such as the police or child protective services. This is to protect both you and others from further abuse.

Regardless of your age, if you answered any of these items with a score of 2 or higher, you may still need to talk to a professional about those experiences and how they have affected your self-esteem, emotional health, and attitudes about marriage and family life. I suggest discussing this with a parent and then a therapist (Chapter Eight includes a list of organizations that can refer you to a licensed therapist in your area) or clergy person first. Therapists, especially, can assist you in evaluating how these experiences may have affected you and your marital aptitude. A clergy person or therapist can also help you understand state laws and ethical requirements involved in reporting abuse to the authorities, protecting other family members from abuse, and getting professional help for the abuser.

If you are a victim of childhood physical, sexual, or emotional abuse, how has this affected your self-esteem? Your emotional health? Your ability to trust others? Attitudes and feelings about marriage? About sex?

_____

_____

_____

_____

_____

_____

After processing your thoughts and feelings about your past abuse, get a professional opinion as to when to discuss these experiences with your partner. An experienced therapist can help you decide what information to share or keep private.

Parental Mental Health

Look at your answer to item 23 in Exhibit 3.1. If your answer was 3 or higher, these parental emotional problems may have affected you in a significant way while you were growing up. If your score was 3 or higher, answer these questions for yourself and discuss your answers as appropriate with your partner. If a parent experienced a serious mental health problem or addiction, how did those experiences affect you as a child? How do they affect you now? How do you think they will affect your marriage?

_____

_____

_____

_____

_____

_____

Family Status

Look at your answer to item 24 in Exhibit 3.1. If your parents divorced, answer these questions:

• How did their divorce affect you emotionally as a child? How does it affect you now?

_____

_____

_____

- How has their divorce affected your attitudes about

  Marriage (for example, At what age should you marry? What are the benefits of marriage? What are the costs?)
  Commitment?
  Trusting a member of the opposite sex?
  Divorce as a solution to marriage problems?

  _____

  _____

  _____

  _____

- How has your parents' divorce affected your communication and conflict resolution skills?

  _____

  _____

  _____

If one or both parents died before you were eighteen, how has that affected you emotionally? If you lived with a stepparent, what was your relationship with that parent like? How has that relationship affected your attitudes and feelings about yourself and marriage? If you lived with a foster family or a relative, how has that affected you emotionally? How has it affected your attitudes and feelings about yourself and marriage? If you were adopted, write answers to the same questions in this paragraph.

_____

_____

_____

_____

_____

_____

Discuss your answers to these important questions about family status with your partner when you feel comfortable doing so. Ask your partner to consider these questions too and talk to you about the attitudes and feelings they evoke.

Overall, what are your unique assets or strengths as identified in this chapter? Why? What are your unique liabilities or weaknesses? What can you do to improve in these areas? For example, if your father-child relationship was poor, what can you do to improve it now? How? If your family processes were dysfunctional, what can you do to overcome the influence of these processes on you now?

_____

_____

_____

_____

_____

_____

In Chapter Eight you will find recommended self-help books for overcoming dysfunctional family processes. Remember, no one has a perfect background for marriage! All of us have strengths and weaknesses from our past that affect our current relationships. It's how you resolve your problems that counts the most in marriage preparation. Don't let problem relationships from the past overcome you and cause problems in your current relationship. If necessary, seek the assistance of caring friends, family members, clergy persons, or a professional therapist to help you overcome the emotional pain or negative attitudes associated with dysfunctional family process experiences. It is important to resolve old issues from the past so they will not interfere with your personal happiness or your future marital satisfaction.

Personal Characteristics

Look at your responses to items 25–30 in Exhibit 3.1. Based on what you have learned in this chapter, how will each of these factors be either an asset for you (for example, older age at marriage) or a liability for you (for example, younger age at marriage)? How can you turn your liabilities into assets (for example, waiting until you're older to get married)?

_____

_____

_____

_____

_____

_____

Parents' or Friends' Approval

The items in this section deal with your relationship contexts including approval of your marriage and pressure to get married. First, look at your scores on items 31–36 in Exhibit 3.1. Write the names of people for whom you circled an answer of 1 or 2 on these items here:

1. _____   4. _____

2. _____   5. _____

3. _____   6. _____

These are important individuals in your social context who either do *not* approve of your marriage or who have doubts.

Individuals whom you scored a 3 or 4 are the opposite—they mostly or entirely approve of your marriage. Now write the names of people for whom you circled an answer of 3 or 4 on items 31–36 here:

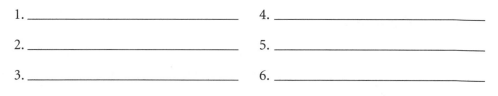

1. _____   4. _____

2. _____   5. _____

3. _____   6. _____

For those who approve, answer this question: Why do they approve? What feedback have they given you that makes you feel more confident about this relationship? For those who do not approve, what are their concerns? Have you given their concerns enough serious thought? Have you and your partner discussed their objections? Why or why not? What do you need to do next?

_____

_____

_____

_____

_____

_____

_____

Internal and External Pressure

Now, look at your response to item 37 in Exhibit 3.1. Who is moving faster in your relationship? Is someone moving too fast for comfort or wisdom? If so, why? What are the advantages and disadvantages of going so fast? Of slowing down? Now, look at your response to item 38—if you answered it with a 2 or 3, discuss this pressure with your partner. How might this pressure interfere with your getting better acquainted before marriage? How else does this pressure negatively affect you and your relationship?

If you feel no pressure to get married, celebrate! That's one less stressor on your relationship and marriage decision.

Overall, are your relationship contexts an asset or liability for your marriage? Why? What can you do now to turn liabilities into assets (for example, wait until you are older, have a better job, or have parental approval before marrying)? What are your unique relationship context assets? How will they improve your chances of marital satisfaction? Discuss your answers to all of these questions with your partner.

Recommendations

Try to get your parents' and friends' approval for your marriage. *Go slow* if they do not support you now—they may support you later. By going slow you show them you respect their opinions. However, ultimately marriage is your decision. If you feel that these loved ones never approve of any serious relationship you have, it may be that they just do not want to let go of you emotionally and no one will ever be worthy of marrying you as far as they're concerned. In this case, you may want to take their objections less seriously. If in doubt, discuss this with a more objective person (for example, a trusted friend, clergy person, or therapist).

If you're feeling undue pressure to marry, uncover the reason for it now. Face your doubts, feelings of intimidation by others, guilt trips others may be placing on you, manipulation by others, threats, or whatever. Simply stated, marriage is not a decision that you should make under pressure—external or internal pressure. Refuse to move forward with marriage plans until you have faced the pressure monster and defeated it. You will not be sorry!

Congratulations! You have now finished assessing the first factor in the Marriage Triangle! The next chapter discusses how your individual traits such as personality are related to later marital satisfaction. It also gives you the opportunity to assess select personality traits and personal characteristics in this context. Continue to be open-minded and honest in answering those questions and discussing the results with your partner.

FOUR

The Marriage Triangle, Factor 2

Your Individual Traits

He had a bad temper, he was power-oriented and controlling. I really thought that he would abuse me or my children if I married him. He didn't respect my body because of his temper.

—Emily, twenty-year-old college student

My self-esteem was so low that I just "had to have him" even though deep down I knew we were not well-matched.

—Kate, twenty-five-year-old accountant

I love her and I hope she will change. She has poor self-esteem. If there's any discussion of problems in our relationship, she puts up defenses and throws everything back or says she is worthless.

—Russ, twenty-five-year-old graduate student

We were very in love, but we had a lot of differences in what we valued and how we wanted to live our lives. Also, his upbringing and attitudes toward women were not the same as mine. It took me a long time to realize these things because I loved him so much.

—Patricia, twenty-four-year-old insurance adjuster

I think I sometimes put too much stress on her—you know, always asking for favors. But, wow! She can handle it!

—Jack, twenty-nine-year-old Realtor

He is so flexible whenever I suggest a change. I don't feel like we always have to do things *his* way.

—Carol, twenty-one-year-old massage therapist

I'm glad my self-esteem is good enough that I can handle all the attention other men give to her when we're out. It would be real easy for most men to get jealous in those situations.

—Paul, twenty-three-year-old college student

These statements by single adults show how individual traits may contribute negatively or positively to an intimate relationship and either encourage or discourage people from getting married. The major purpose of this chapter is to help you understand how certain individual traits in you and your partner affect the way you relate to each other, handle stress, become more intimate, and eventually create marital satisfaction or dissatisfaction. In this chapter I use research to answer two important questions:

- What personality traits or interpersonal skills are related to either marital satisfaction or dissatisfaction?
- What types of functional and dysfunctional beliefs are related to satisfaction or dissatisfaction?

Individual traits are an important leg of the Marriage Triangle (see Figure 2.1). Without good mental health and certain personality characteristics, you or your partner may be a spouse who is hard to live with. As marital expert Lawrence Kurdek said so well, "Personality traits may predispose a partner to distort relationship events or to overreact to negative relationship events. Certain traits may contribute to the partner's being someone with whom it is very difficult to live."[1]

Let me share an example of this. Stacey (twenty) had low self-esteem including a poor body image, self-doubt, and self-consciousness. She reacted negatively to many things that happened with her boyfriend, Jim (twenty-one). For example, if he forgot to call her, she would have all kinds of negative thoughts about it—"He must not really love me or he would call. I'm obviously not a priority in his life. I wonder if he is with another girl!" These kinds of escalating negative thoughts or self-statements are distortions of reality. However, as a result, she would pounce on Jim when he finally did call the next day, inappropriately accusing him of being with another girl. In reality, he had slept all day because he was sick! She felt guilty when she found out. As you can imagine, Jim was increasingly finding Stacey a difficult person to be with!

Individual traits are like the nucleus of a cell (recall Figure 2.2 for couple traits). They are essential for having a healthy couple relationship and relating successfully to the contexts described in Chapter Three. For example, if I have good self-esteem, I will deal better with the stress of parental approval issues (context), problems stemming from my family of origin like parental divorce (context), and will communicate more directly and clearly with my partner (couple trait) than if I have poor self-esteem. Before going any further, let's do an assessment of some of your key individual traits. Please complete and score the short tests in Exhibit 4.1. At the end of the chapter I'll help you interpret the meanings of these scores.

✂ Personality Traits Related to Marital Satisfaction

Now let's answer the questions posed at the beginning of the chapter. First, what personality traits does research show are related to later marital dissatisfaction when taken to excess? Here they are:

Individual Traits That Predict Marital Dissatisfaction

- Vulnerability to stress
- Impulsiveness
- Anger and hostility
- Depression
- Anxiety
- Self-consciousness
- Dysfunctional beliefs

	Never	Rarely	Sometimes	Often	Very Often
					Circle your responses:

Personality Traits

Answer how well these words describe you now:

	Never	Rarely	Sometimes	Often	Very Often
1. Talkative	1	2	3	4	5
2. Quiet	1	2	3	4	5
3. Shy	1	2	3	4	5
4. Outgoing	1	2	3	4	5

Reverse-score items 2 and 3. (See first section of Exhibit 3.1 for directions.)
Then, sum your responses to items 1–4 and write your score here: _____

	Never	Rarely	Sometimes	Often	Very Often
5. Worried	1	2	3	4	5
6. Fearful	1	2	3	4	5
7. Tense	1	2	3	4	5
8. Nervous	1	2	3	4	5

Sum your responses to items 5–8 and write your score here: _____

	Never	Rarely	Sometimes	Often	Very Often
9. Open minded	1	2	3	4	5
10. Flexible	1	2	3	4	5
11. Easy going	1	2	3	4	5
12. Adaptable	1	2	3	4	5

Sum your responses to items 9–12 and write your score here: _____

	Never	Rarely	Sometimes	Often	Very Often
13. Fight with others, lose temper	1	2	3	4	5
14. Act immature under pressures	1	2	3	4	5
15. Easily irritated or mad	1	2	3	4	5

Sum your responses to items 13–15 and write your score here: _____

Exhibit 4.1. Assessing Personality Traits

Note: Items 37–51 used by permission of Taylor & Francis Publications.[2]

	Never	Rarely	Sometimes	Often	Very Often
					Circle your responses:
16. Sad and blue	1	2	3	4	5
17. Hopeless	1	2	3	4	5
18. Depressed	1	2	3	4	5

Sum your responses to items 16–18 and write your score here: _____

	Never	Rarely	Sometimes	Often	Very Often
19. Impulsive	1	2	3	4	5
20. Act before thinking first	1	2	3	4	5
21. Easily tempted	1	2	3	4	5

Sum your responses to items 19–21 and write your score here: _____

	Never	Rarely	Sometimes	Often	Very Often
22. Deal well with stress	1	2	3	4	5
23. Fall apart in a crisis	1	2	3	4	5
24. Helpless under pressure	1	2	3	4	5

Reverse-score item 22. Then sum your responses to items 22–24 and write your score here: _____

	Never	Rarely	Sometimes	Often	Very Often
25. Speak up in a crowd	1	2	3	4	5
26. Tell it like it is	1	2	3	4	5
27. Say what I really think	1	2	3	4	5
28. Assertive	1	2	3	4	5

Sum your responses to items 25–28 and write your score here: _____

	Never	Rarely	Sometimes	Often	Very Often
29. Take a positive attitude toward myself	1	2	3	4	5
30. Think I am not good at all	1	2	3	4	5
31. Feel I am a person of worth	1	2	3	4	5
32. Think I am a failure	1	2	3	4	5

Reverse-score items 30 and 32. Then sum your responses to items 29–32 and write your score here: _____

Exhibit 4.1. *Continued*

33. My partner or I have an emotional or personal problem that should be treated by a professional—depression, phobia, anxiety, eating disorder, or some such. Circle your response: YES NO (UNSURE)

34. My partner or I have serious, chronic physical health problems that should be treated by a professional—ulcer, diabetes, a handicap, chronic fatigue, or some such. Circle your response: YES (NO) UNSURE

Beliefs About Individuals or Relationships

Rate the extent to which you agree with the following statements.

	Strongly Disagree	Disagree	Undecided	Agree	Strongly Agree
35. Time will resolve any problems we have as a couple.	1	2	3	4	5
36. There are many things about my partner I would like to change after marriage.	1	2	3	4	5
37. If your partner disagrees with your ideas, he or she probably does not think highly of you.	1	2	3	4	5
38. I cannot accept it when my partner disagrees with me.	1	2	3	4	5
39. I take it as a personal insult when my partner disagrees with an important idea of mine.	1	2	3	4	5

Sum your responses to items 37–39 and write your score here: _____

(Note: Do not include items 35 and 36 in this sum.)

| 40. I get very upset if my partner does not recognize how I am feeling and I have to tell him or her. | 1 | 2 | 3 | 4 | 5 |

Exhibit 4.1. *Continued*

Rate the extent to which you agree with the following statements.

	Strongly Disagree	Disagree	Undecided	Agree	Strongly Agree
41. People who have a close relationship can sense each other's needs as if they could read each other's minds.	1	2	3	4	5
42. It is important to me for my partner to anticipate my needs by sensing changes in my moods.	1	2	3	4	5

Sum your responses to items 40–42 and write your score here: _____

	Strongly Disagree	Disagree	Undecided	Agree	Strongly Agree
43. My partner does not seem capable of behaving other than he or she does now.	1	2	3	4	5
44. A partner who hurts you badly once will probably hurt you again.	1	2	3	4	5
45. I do not expect my partner to be able to change.	1	2	3	4	5

Sum your responses to items 43–45 and write your score here: _____

	Strongly Disagree	Disagree	Undecided	Agree	Strongly Agree
46. A good sexual partner can get himself or herself aroused for sex whenever necessary.	1	2	3	4	5
47. If I cannot perform well sexually whenever my partner is in the mood, I would consider that I have a problem.	1	2	3	4	5
48. Some difficulties in my sexual performance mean personal failure to me.	1	2	3	4	5

Sum your responses to items 46–48 and write your score here: _____

	Strongly Disagree	Disagree	Undecided	Agree	Strongly Agree
49. Misunderstandings between partners generally are due to inborn differences in the psychological makeup of men and women.	1	2	3	4	5

Exhibit 4.1. *Continued*

Rate the extent to which you agree with the following statements.

	Strongly Disagree	Disagree	Undecided	Agree	Strongly Agree
50. You can't really understand someone of the opposite sex.	1	2	3	4	5
51. One of the major causes of marital problems is that men and women have different emotional needs.	1	2	3	4	5

Sum your responses to items 49–51 and write your score here: _____

Exhibit 4.1. *Continued*

Predictable Problems

The first six personality traits on the list are called *neurotic traits.*[3] All of us have some degree of each of these traits—that's normal. What is not normal is for you or your partner to have excessive amounts of those traits on a regular basis. Individuals who do have these traits on a regular basis find life difficult most of the time and have a relatively negative view of self, others, and the world. It should be easy to see how excessive amounts of these traits can spoil a marriage. Let's look at some examples.

Marriage is frequently stressful. After all, you live with another person with a unique personality and hang-ups. Then there are the stresses of adjusting to each other's quirks, habits, and needs. You have to work out your husband and wife roles. You coordinate your busy lives every day. You have to solve conflicts and make important decisions. The list goes on! Is it any wonder that good stress management is an asset for you in marriage?

Those with excessive, chronic anxiety are miserable and are difficult to live with. They seldom relax. They often do not enjoy sex. They are not fun to be around most of the time.

Excessive irritability, anger, or hostility poisons any relationship—especially marriage. An irritable or angry person wears out their partner. Often anger and anxiety go together. For example, Lana (twenty-three) was a worrywart. She just couldn't turn off the worry. If it wasn't bills she worried about, it was her health, school assignments, work, her mother's health problems. . . . The list was endless! Ron (twenty-five) constantly tried to calm her down and reassure her that all was well. It didn't work. This free-floating anxiety and irritability caused Lana to criticize Ron frequently and unfairly. She picked at the way he dressed, cleaned their apartment, and paid the bills. He felt he could not come home without being chewed out as soon as he walked through the door.

Excessive depression affects marriage on many fronts. Activities together—there are fewer; sex—there is less; managing the house—only one partner does most of the work; making decisions—it doesn't get done in a timely way. It's easy to see how depressing it would be to live with a person with chronic depression!

Being impulsive occasionally is fun—but it doesn't take much to be too much. For example, leaving my office at the spur of the moment to play golf is great sometimes! After all, you can't plan *all* of your week. However, if I act impulsively too often, my job suffers, my boss is displeased, and my wife is angry. Impulsive spending is perhaps the most dangerous kind of impulsive behavior in marriage. It can lead to resentment from your spouse, who is trying to restrict spending for the sake of the family budget, and it can lead to marital conflict, guilt on your part, stress on the marriage, and sometimes financial ruin. Skip (thirty) and Roxanne (twenty-six) told me a story related to this. Just before they married they were struggling to save as much money as possible. One Saturday Skip presented Roxanne with a new, expensive mountain bike that he had purchased on sale. His reasoning was, "What the heck, you needed one! It's summer!" The salesperson had talked him into a variety of accessories, too. This decision was certainly kind and generous—but irresponsible and impulsive as well. He returned the bike three days later after an intense argument with Roxanne about his impulsiveness. Roxanne started worrying that he might make the same kind of snap decisions after they were married. She was angry with him for over a week!

Low self-esteem and high self-consciousness tend to frustrate people and drive them away. If you sincerely compliment someone with these traits ("You look great today!"), they usually dismiss it ("Oh, I just threw on the first clothes I could find!"). I call these people *approval types.* They seem to need approval constantly. The truth is, complimenting them is not the solution. Praise and feedback from others doesn't help much. Their problem comes from within. These individuals hold negative views of themselves and others. They think negatively. They are pessimists. They wear us out!

Notice that many of these six traits go together in the same individuals. For example, depressed people usually have low self-esteem and are anxious. They often are vulnerable to stress. And someone who doesn't handle stress well may become irritable, angry, and hostile. These emotions are understandably linked together.

Let me reiterate that low or even occasionally moderate levels of these neurotic traits are part of being a normal human being. To some degree, neurotic is normal! It's when these traits are exaggerated for long periods of time that we need to be concerned. At the end of this chapter I will explain how to determine if your scores on these traits are especially high and what to do if they are.

Let's turn now to individual traits that are related to later marital satisfaction. First, we can say that an absence or low level of the neurotic traits just discussed will help you have greater marital satisfaction. But what other traits will help you cope with the stresses of marriage?

Individual Traits That Predict Marital Satisfaction

- Extroversion
- Flexibility
- Assertiveness

A More Positive Prediction

Extroverts or individuals high in sociability tend to like people and like being around people. They tend to be assertive, active, and talkative. They usually have a cheerful disposition and are upbeat, energetic, and optimistic. These traits together with flexibility make you or your partner a relatively easy person to get along with. Nanette (twenty-five) described Stephan (twenty-five) that way: "Stephan is easy to talk to, he usually tells me what he wants [that is, he's assertive], but if I want just the opposite of what he wants, he can compromise. The other day we were debating which kind of car to buy. Rather than just shrugging his shoulders when I asked what he wanted, he emphasized his need to have a vehicle that he could drive off-road. I wanted great gas mileage. Then he bought home a huge, gas-eating 4x4 truck he sounded sold on. But after hearing my needs he (somewhat reluctantly) took the truck back to the dealer. A week later we settled for a four-wheel-drive economy station wagon and both of us were happy!"

Flexibility is important because of the myriad unforeseen changes, events, disappointments, and miscalculations we make in life. In contrast, rigid people more often end up frustrated and angry because they can't have their way. They are more difficult to get along with and resolving differences is sometimes impossible.

As mentioned earlier, assertiveness is the honest and open communication of one's thoughts, feelings, and needs. Imagine how difficult it would be to discuss marital issues or even make simple decisions with a partner who is nonassertive! The conversation might sound like this:

ASSERTIVE SPOUSE: I'd like to go to the show tonight. I heard there's a good double feature downtown that sounds good to me. What do you think?

NONASSERTIVE SPOUSE *(in a spiteful tone)*: I don't know. Whatever you say usually goes anyway.

ASSERTIVE SPOUSE: That's not true! You just never seem to be able to make a simple decision. But I'm really interested in how you feel about this since if we go to a double feature we will get home late. Would that bother you?

NONASSERTIVE SPOUSE: I don't know. *You* decide.

This is a crazy-making conversation! The problem with nonassertive partners is they frequently defer to you for an opinion or decision. They often do not think that their opinion is important or valued. Basically, they think others' needs are more important than their needs. They avoid rocking the boat. They chronically fail to get their needs met in a relationship and leave their partners mystified about what's going on inside them. Later, they may explode over minor problems, when their level of suppressed frustration overflows.

In summary, more sociable, flexible, and assertive people have a higher marital aptitude than less sociable, flexible, and assertive people. And less neurotic people have a higher marital aptitude than more neurotic people. Fortunately, most of these individual traits individuals bring with them into marriage can be modified. For example, assertiveness training helps nonassertive individuals learn to speak up. Most of us can learn to be more flexible and sociable. Neurotic traits can be modified through self-help processes (books, tapes, workshops) as well as professional therapy. The message here: You *can* improve individual traits that will increase your marital aptitude and readiness. It takes humility, self-awareness, and effort. But it can be done! And the best time to work on yourself is *before* marriage. Remember this important statement:[4]

> MARRIAGE IS *NOT* A MAGICAL CURE
> FOR PERSONAL PROBLEMS....
>
> MARRIAGE ONLY *INTENSIFIES*
> PERSONAL PROBLEMS!!!

Dysfunctional Beliefs Related to Marital Dissatisfaction

Researchers have identified several types of dysfunctional beliefs about individuals and relationships that predict marital dissatisfaction.[5] These beliefs are usually held before marriage and are taken into the marriage, where they cause problems. Beliefs are important because they form the basis for how we feel and behave. For example, if my wife forgot to buy me a birthday gift, I might choose to believe any of the following things:

1. She is really busy or stressed—no wonder she forgot!
2. She doesn't love me anymore.
3. She is a thoughtless and selfish person who should be punished.
4. She has a poor memory for important dates.

If I choose belief number 1 or 4, I will probably be less upset and less likely to criticize her than if I choose belief number 2 or 3.

You may hold select dysfunctional beliefs about marriage or your partner that will result in frustration and disappointment for you and ultimately in negative behavior on your part toward your spouse. Such dysfunctional beliefs can be categorized as follows:

Marriage will bring magical change. These are beliefs that time will solve any problems you have as a couple and that your partner will change dramatically after you've married. Unfortunately, neither is realistic!

Disagreement is destructive. Beliefs such as "disagreement means you have a bad marriage" or "disagreements will destroy your marriage" are unrealistic. They will keep you as a couple from facing areas of disagreement in marriage and resolving them.

Mind reading is expected. This includes beliefs such as "If you really loved me, you would automatically know what I need to be happy" or "You should know what I want without my saying it." This is also referred to as the ESP myth. Unfortunately, most of us cannot read our partner's mind. Instead, we expect our partner to tell us what he or she needs or wants.

A partner cannot change. Examples of this belief include statements like "People don't really change all that much over time," or "My partner is incapable of change!" Such beliefs inhibit us from asking our partner for change and lead to discouragement, frustration, and resentment. Fortunately, people *can* and *do* change!

Sexual perfection is possible. Beliefs such as "There is one right way to have sex," or "Only if we both achieve orgasm at the same time can we be satisfied" are examples of this type of perfectionism. More realistically, we are all fallible human beings—things don't always go the way we would like. In fact, seldom do things go perfectly! That doesn't mean we cannot enjoy sex very much even when things are not perfect.

The sexes are completely different. These beliefs are that "Men and women are mysteriously different from each other" and that "Men and women will never really understand each other." Such inaccurate beliefs discourage us from understanding, appreciating, and adapting to each other's similarities and differences.

All six types of beliefs described above are dysfunctional because they are constraining. "Constraining beliefs perpetuate problems and restrict options for alternative solutions to problems. Facilitative (or functional) beliefs increase options for solutions to problems."[6] For example, if you believe that the sexes are greatly and mysteriously different (as described above), you will be constrained in solving marital problems. Such a belief will lead to frustration and problems described like this:

- It's no use! I'll never understand her. So, why even try?

- Men! No one knows how to please them!

- No, I will *not* participate in that communication enhancement program. It's no use trying to figure out what's going on in your head!

- She's so different from me that I'll just have to live my life my own way and hope it doesn't cause too many waves in our marriage.

A more facilitative or functional belief about differences between the sexes might be: "Men and women are different, but social scientists know a lot more today about those differences and can show us how to appreciate and manage our differences," or, "Men and women are more alike than different—and the differences are less mysterious since social scientists have begun studying them." These last two beliefs are also supported by research.

At the end of this chapter I'll make recommendations on how you can challenge and change dysfunctional beliefs to more functional ones. For now, let's look at how you scored on the individual traits items you responded to at the beginning of the chapter.

🎱 Scoring and Interpretation Guidelines: Individual Traits

The traits you assessed at the beginning of the chapter are divided into these three major sections: personality traits, interpersonal skills (such as assertiveness), and other personal problems and dysfunctional beliefs.

Personality Traits

The first short tests you took were brief measures of personality traits shown to predict either marital dissatisfaction or satisfaction. Look back at Exhibit 4.1 for your sum scores for each short test and enter your sum scores in the spaces provided in Exhibit 4.2.

Interpretation Guidelines

Let's look first at your perceptions of your personality traits that are predictors of marital dissatisfaction. These are your liabilities or areas that need improvement before marriage. Compare your scores with the norm scores on the following short tests:

- Anxiety
- Anger and hostility
- Depression
- Impulsivity
- Vulnerability to stress

Norm scores refer to the average score for over five thousand individuals age seventeen through thirty who have completed these short tests from the RELATE

Extroversion Sum Score (items 1–4):   _____

      Range of scores: 4–20   Norm score: 14.0

Anxiety Sum Score (items 5–8):   _____

      Range of scores: 4–20   Norm score: 11.0

Flexibility Sum Score (items 9–12):   _____

      Range of scores: 4–20   Norm score: 16.2

Anger and Hostility Sum Score (items 13–15):   _____

      Range of scores: 3–15   Norm score: 6.6

Depression Sum Score (items 16–18):   _____

      Range of scores: 3–15   Norm score: 6.7

Impulsivity Sum Score (items 19–21):   _____

      Range of scores: 3–15   Norm score: 9.5

Vulnerability to Stress Sum Score (items 22–24):   _____

      Range of scores: 3–15   Norm score: 9.3

Assertiveness Sum Score (items 25–28):   _____

      Range of scores: 4–20   Norm score: 10.5

Self-Esteem Sum Score (items 29–32):   _____

      Range of scores: 4–20   Norm score: 17.2

Exhibit 4.2. Personality Assessment Summary

instrument over the last two years. By comparing your scores to these national norm scores, you will understand how similar or different you are to others.

If your score on anxiety is 2 points or more above the norm score for anxiety, your score is considered "high." This means you are significantly more anxious than the individuals in the norm group who have taken the RELATE. If your score is at or below the norm score, you are considered to have average or below average anxiety. So how does your score compare? If you are high on anxiety, what is the cause? What can you do to become less anxious? The higher your score on anxiety, the more likely you are to benefit from self-help books or professional therapy for anxiety reduction. Books recommended for anxiety reduction are described in Chapter Eight. A therapist referral guide is also described there.

Now compare your results on the other short tests with the norm scores from the RELATE. For these personality traits, a score of 2 or more points *above* the norm scores should be considered a "high" score. So how do your scores compare with the norm scores? If your scores are about at the norm or lower, these personality traits should not be considered areas of needed improvement for you—you're probably no more angry, impulsive, or the rest than the average single young adult. Great! As with anxiety, if you have a high score on one of these traits, ask yourself, What is the cause? For example, if your depression score is higher than average, what is going on in your life right now that is causing you to feel so low? For the others, what is causing your anger? What problems are impulsivity causing for you? What makes it difficult for you to cope with stress? More important, what can you do now to become less depressed, less angry or impulsive, and cope better with stress? (Self-help resources and guidelines for therapy are to be found in Chapter Eight.)

_____

_____

_____

_____

_____

Now the good news! With good self-help literature, support from your loved ones, and in some cases therapy, you can overcome these problems—even though, if left untreated, they may inhibit your ability to have a satisfying marriage. Please note that the short tests used in this book should not be considered as comprehensive evaluations of these personality traits. If as a result of taking these short tests you are concerned that you may be seriously depressed, impulsive, angry, or whatever, consult with a therapist who can assist you with further detailed testing, a psychological interview, and a diagnosis as necessary. High scores on the short tests in this book should only be considered as warning signs that should direct you to a deeper analysis of your problems and their solutions.

Whew! The hardest part is over! Now, let's look at the personality traits that predict marital satisfaction. These are resources or assets that you take into marriage. These traits are

- Extroversion
- Flexibility
- Assertiveness
- Self-esteem

Compare your scores with the norm scores. If your scores on any of these short tests are 2 points or more *lower* than the norm scores, your scores are considered "low." If your scores are 2 points or more *higher* than the norm scores, they are considered "high." Higher scores reflect more positive personality traits related to later marital satisfaction.

So what are your highest scores? A score can be considered as an asset if it is at or above the norm score. Liabilities are represented by traits where you scored low. What traits need improvement? What can you do *now* to improve? Self-help and therapy suggestions on how to improve these traits are given in Chapter Eight.

_____

_____

_____

_____

_____

_____

Should We Stay Together?

More Specific Guidelines on Personality Traits

If you scored high on depression and anxiety, you may expect to score low on self-esteem. As mentioned earlier, these three traits are closely related. Since difficulties with these traits are so commonly experienced by American young adults, let me say a few important things about them.

First, if you have problems in one or more of these three areas, get a more thorough psychological evaluation by a therapist. You may have clinical depression, that is, more serious depression than the normal blues. You may be depressed enough to benefit from therapy or medication.

Second, most people who suffer from depression don't even know it! There is nothing shameful about having depression. It is the common cold of psychological problems. It is estimated that over 15 percent of all Americans will be affected with this syndrome sometime during their lives. This means clinical depression affects 100 million people worldwide every day.[7] In addition to anxiety, depressed mood, and low self-esteem, individuals with this syndrome may experience appetite loss, apathy, hopelessness, sleep problems, difficulty making decisions, and loss of interest in previously pleasurable things or activities. See your physician or therapist for a more complete evaluation.

Third, you may not have clinical depression but you may be suffering from an anxiety disorder. These syndromes, like depression, can be effectively diagnosed and treated by a physician or therapist.

Fourth, with all the excellent therapy and medication resources available today for the treatment of depression and anxiety, you should not let ignorance or pride stand in the way of your feeling better. Be smart—like a college couple I once counseled who were strongly considering marriage. Both partners were mildly depressed, but loved each other and were otherwise well-matched. I suggested that they first "get healthy" and then consider marriage more seriously. Depression was making it difficult for them to decide if they should marry. Shortly after seeing me, they separated to their home towns for the summer. After three months of therapy and taking an antidepressant medication, the man's depression was largely cured. The woman got better, too. They met back at school, at which point they could see their future more clearly—and decided not to marry. Eighteen months later he married another woman and now has two children. They are happy, too, and he has not experienced any further bouts of depression. I lost touch with the woman who consulted me with him, but hope she had an equally bright future!

Improving Self-Esteem

Perhaps you are not especially depressed or anxious but still have low self-esteem. Neil Warren suggests some ways to improve your esteem:

Find a source of unconditional love from a trusted friend, relative, clergy person, or therapist. Elicit from them feedback that will build you up and encourage you. This suggestion worked for me when I was a twenty-two-year-old college student dating a twenty-year-old girl whom I never felt secure with due to my own low self-esteem. I sought the advice of an older, more mature friend whose judgment I trusted concerning our relationship. First, he reassured me that I was a person of worth. He also gently confronted me. His observation was that I needed to improve my self-esteem but that I also should get out of this relationship—my girlfriend was dragging down my self-esteem even more by her erratic behavior toward me. Looking back, he was right on both counts. We broke up and I eventually felt better about myself. I learned to better recognize the kinds of relationships that would not damage my self-esteem.

"Learn to love yourself."[8] For many this may be learned through self-help books, which I recommend in Chapter Eight. For others, therapy will be necessary. This suggestion holds the most promise and power for helping you improve your self-esteem.

Other Emotional Problems and Physical Health

Look at your responses to items 33 and 34 in Exhibit 4.1. What emotional or physical problems do either of you have that may negatively affect your marriage? For example, Brett (twenty-four) and Megan (twenty-five) were just about engaged to be married when he was diagnosed with a serious and chronic health problem. Both worried about how this physical health problem would affect their marriage. How would it affect his ability to make a living? To get health insurance and life insurance? Have normal sexual relations? Many such important questions arose. After educating themselves about the disease and its control, much individual thought and reflection, many discussions together, seeking advice from trusted parents and clergy, and prayer, the couple decided to pursue the marriage after all. They are happily married one year later principally as a result of going into the marriage with their eyes wide open and with expectations that were reasonable. For example, Megan realizes she is likely to be a widow earlier than most married women. She knows she will probably need to work outside the family for most of their marriage for the couple to afford the expensive health insurance, medications, tests, and treatment required by his disease. To her credit, she was willing to do all these things to be Brett's wife.

A second engaged couple once saw me for counseling, complaining that Janet (twenty) had unexplainable mood swings that exasperated both of them. These swings seemed more serious than the normal highs and lows most of us experience. Janet's diagnosis was Bipolar Disorder—sometimes called manic depression. Some days she would be on top of the world—full of boundless energy, often staying up forty-eight hours straight with no sleep. She had grandiose ideas that she was Superwoman and "the greatest lover he had ever known." In this manic state, she was wearing out Thad (twenty-two) physically and emotionally. Then, suddenly, she would crash and burn. She was depressed, had difficulty getting out of bed in the morning, felt hopeless about the future, and lost all her interest in sex or him. At this point she had symptoms of clinical depression that would last for several weeks before she would spin out of control again with her mania.

She was treated with medication and therapy—both individual and couple therapy. Her condition significantly improved. Her boyfriend learned how to give her constructive feedback on her moods, help her stay on the medication (which is crucial in the treatment of Bipolar Disorder), be more understanding, and help her control the stress in her life. As a result, they are now happily married.

The important principle in both of these cases is the same: Get diagnosis and treatment *before* you marry!! It will make the challenging adjustments to marriage in the first few years easier and ultimately result in a longer, happier marriage. So, if you answered "Undecided," "Agree" or "Strongly Agree" to question 33 or 34, slow down and thoughtfully consider what to do next. Seek first for a professional diagnosis. Then learn all you can about the problem and its solutions. Do as these wise couples did and first take private time to consider what to do and couple time for long discussions and decision making. Don't deny or minimize these problems or think that magically, "Love will conquer all!" It takes much more than that to have a satisfying marriage.

8 Dysfunctional Beliefs That Influence Marital Satisfaction

Earlier you assessed how much you agreed with several types of beliefs about yourself, your partner, and marriage that predict later marital dissatisfaction. First, look at your scores on items 35 and 36 in Exhibit 4.1. Did you circle "Agree" or "Strongly Agree" for either item? If so, you have unrealistic expectations about marriage! Please consider these two points:

Time alone does not solve most marriage problems; rather, a solution takes hard work, unselfishness, good communication skills, and commitment. Fifty years of research shows this!

You cannot change someone else! But you can change your own attitudes, behaviors, and habits. Pointing out your partner's inadequacies, repeated reminders, nagging, threatening, and so on never work. These strategies only create power struggles. In addition, if you already recognize things about your partner that you don't like and hope will change, why are you magically thinking that he or she will more easily hear your feedback or change after the wedding? What is keeping you from confronting these issues *now*? If you wait until after the wedding to confront these issues, your spouse is likely to respond: "You knew I had these problems before you married me, so don't gripe about them now!" or "You need to accept me for who I am."

I would even argue that your feedback will find a better chance of acceptance before marriage than after marriage. This is because before marriage your partner is especially trying to please you and respond to your requests. So use this period of time wisely. Engagement is not only a joyous time, it is also a time to look more deeply at ourselves, resolve differences, and make personal or couple changes that are reasonable. However, if there is too long a list of such changes, perhaps you are not ready to get married or are poorly matched and should not pursue marriage.

The Myth of Perfect Harmony

Now, let's look at your responses to other dysfunctional beliefs. Check your score on items 37–39 in Exhibit 4.1. High scores on this scale are 7.0 or above. A high score means you believe that disagreements in marriage are destructive. Fortunately, they usually are not nor do they have to be. It depends on how you and your partner resolve them. If you do so by listening to each other respectfully, avoiding criticism and defensiveness, and being willing to compromise when necessary, disagreements actually strengthen a relationship by helping partners understand each other better and feel pride when a disagreement is successfully resolved.

In addition, when couples tell me they have never disagreed it usually means one of the following things:

- They have only known each other for a week.
- They are in denial.
- They are conflict-phobic.
- They never discuss meaningful topics.
- One person is submissive enough to just shut up when disagreements arise.
- They have given up trying to resolve their differences and are hence living in a state of frustration and quiet resentment.
- They are lying to save face.
- Their goal is to get into the *Guinness Book of World Records* as the only couple on earth to never have an argument!

If your score is high on this short test of "disagreement is bad," reconsider your belief. Perhaps you believe conflicts rather than disagreements are bad. Conflict often assumes hot, angry, or out-of-control fights. Is this the case for you? Also, ask yourself these questions:

What is my logic behind this belief? Does it make sense to others when I explain it to them?

What evidence do I have that supports this belief? For example, what have I seen or heard that supports this belief?

Have I observed situations where this belief was challenged? For example, have you ever seen a couple disagree successfully? How did it affect their relationship for the better? When have you seen a couple rigidly avoid disagreements and the relationship suffered?

_____

_____

_____

_____

_____

_____

You needn't rely on your own internal resources and observations. Read good books about how to resolve disagreements successfully in marriage. (See Chapter Eight for several suggestions.) Interview a couple who resolves disagreements successfully and is happily married. How do they do it? What did you learn from them that you can apply in your marriage?

If your score on this short test of disagreements was at or below the norm score, great! This dysfunctional belief will probably not hinder your resolution of disagreements and damage your marital satisfaction.

Now, check your score on items 40–42. A high score (9.0 or above) means you probably believe in ESP—extra-sensory perception. That is, you think people can read each other's minds. If true, this would make communication in marriage unnecessary most of the time. However, there is no scientific evidence for ESP in marriage, even though spouses may become progressively better at guessing what their partner is thinking or wants on occasion. So, speak up about what you think, feel, and want! To challenge your belief in this myth, use the same challenging techniques described earlier for the disagreement belief. If you do not hold the ESP belief, you will be more likely to get your needs met and fulfill your partner's needs in marriage. There will also be fewer misunderstandings.

Adjusting for Differences

Your score on items 43–45 indicates how much you believe that your partner cannot change. A score of 9.0 or more is high. Such a negative view of your partner will result in much frustration and discouragement for both of you. Hope and trust will erode.

The truth is, if people could not change, there would be no need for the millions of therapists and psychiatrists in the world who help millions of people change their lives every day. Change may sometimes be difficult or occur slowly, but it often happens. Coping with the normal stresses of marriage and life will require changes for you and your partner. Don't start off marriage with such a negative, unrealistic, and constraining belief. Ask yourself challenging questions similar to those for the disagreement belief above and you can change this belief to something more realistic, such as "People often change for the better—it's a fortunate part of life and relationships."

What is your score for items 46–48? A high score is 8.5 or more. A high score reflects a "sexual perfectionism" belief. That is, you expect yourself and your partner to perform well under any circumstances. Of course, this is not humanly possible! All of us get tired, stressed out, preoccupied, and so on, and these emotional or physical conditions make it unlikely that we or our partners can perform sexually as we would like to. So, give yourselves a break! Ours is an imperfect world with imperfect people and relationships. Don't expect perfection in your sexual relationship or any other part of your marriage.

Finally, what is your score on the "sexes are different" scale (items 49–51)? A high score is 8.5 or more. If you hold this constraining belief you will fail to solve many marital problems. You may give up even trying to understand your partner. You will take the easy way out and blame a lack of solutions to problems on sex differences rather than a lack of serious effort or skills to resolve differences or understand each other.

Fortunately, men and women are more alike than different, overall.[9] And today, we better understand these differences, know how to adjust to them, and in many cases, make the differences serve as strengths in a marriage.[10] If your score on these items was relatively low, your belief that men and women can understand each other and that differences are mostly learned rather than innate will be a resource to you in marriage.

If your score was high, perhaps you just lack scientific information on sex differences. If so, I recommended reading research-based self-help books on the topic of sex differences in marriage, such as Markman and others' *Fighting for Your Mariage* (see Chapter Eight). Be cautious when reading books based strictly on the author's personal or clinical experiences or observation.

In summary, what are your assets and liabilities in the area of individual traits related to martial satisfaction as outlined in this chapter? List them on the next page:

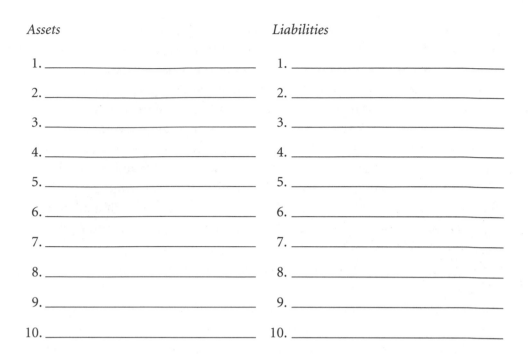

Assets	Liabilities
1. _____	1. _____
2. _____	2. _____
3. _____	3. _____
4. _____	4. _____
5. _____	5. _____
6. _____	6. _____
7. _____	7. _____
8. _____	8. _____
9. _____	9. _____
10. _____	10. _____

What is your ratio of assets to liabilities? Overall, are your individual traits an asset or a liability for you? What does this mean to you? What can you do now to strengthen your individual traits identified in this chapter? Who can help you do this? When will you begin?

_____

_____

_____

_____

_____

_____

_____

_____

Best of luck and congratulations on your assets and willingness to improve yourself before marriage!

We have now assessed two factors in the Marriage Triangle—your individual and relationship contexts and your individual traits. In the next chapter you will learn about and assess couple traits that predict marital satisfaction and dissatisfaction. Continue to be open-minded and honest in answering these questions and discussing the results with your partner.

FIVE

The Marriage Triangle, Factor 3

Your Couple Traits

Brian and I have always loved to talk to each other, and we still do. It seems so easy to open up to each other.

—Jane, twenty-five-year-old graduate student, married one year

Our common bonds are so important to us. We worship together and play together. But most important, our goals are so similar. We seldom fight over where we are going with this marriage.

—Betsy, twenty-seven-year-old nutritionist engaged to a physical therapist

I'm glad I got to know Patricia so well before we committed to a lifetime together. I'm more confident now that it will work.

—Glade, twenty-nine-year-old computer specialist

If you can just sit down and talk and work through problems with respect, you can make a relationship work. Peter and I are proof of that.

—Jessica, twenty-eight-year-old sales representative

These statements reflect the importance of some of the factors in the third and last dimension of the Marriage Triangle, couple traits. This chapter discusses the relationship of the following couple traits to your later marital satisfaction:

- Similarity of your values, attitudes, and backgrounds

- Degree of acquaintanceship before marriage

- Impact of living together on later marital satisfaction

- Impact of premarital sex and pregnancy on later marital satisfaction

- Communication and conflict resolution skills

This chapter differs from its predecessors in that it focuses on your couple relationship rather than on your individual characteristics—your personality or your family background. It answers the following important questions: Which values and attitudes is it important for you and your partner to share in order to achieve marital satisfaction? How long should you know someone before getting married? How will living together affect your chances for a satisfying marriage? How is premarital sex related to later marital satisfaction? If there is a premarital pregnancy, how will it affect your chances of having a satisfying marriage? What couple communication and conflict resolutions skills are important for you to have before marriage?

I have referred to individual traits as being like the nucleus of a cell—Figure 5.1 makes the point again by repeating Figure 2.2.

Couple traits are just as important as the nucleus. In the couple realm, inter-

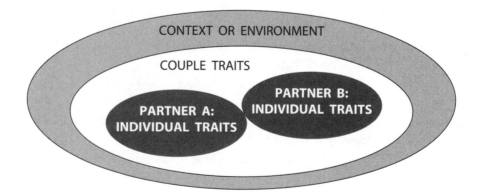

Figure 5.1. Three Levels of a Relationship

action takes place between the two parts of the nucleus—messages are sent, information is received, problems are solved, and so on. Certain characteristics of this realm, called couple traits, affect how well messages are processed and conflicts resolved. For example, if the members of a couple are well-acquainted, are well-matched on values and attitudes, and have good communication skills, communication between them is much easier. If they are not, communication is more difficult, there are more differences to resolve, and in general, life is more stressful. In addition, certain couple dynamics may alter the nature of the couple realm in major ways. These are premarital sex, premarital pregnancy, and living together.

Let's look at an example of how these premarital couple traits intersect to either increase or decrease your chances of later marital satisfaction. Dawn (twenty-two) and Hugh (twenty-four) had "fallen madly in love" in just two months and were already planning a wedding. Their parents were shocked and warned them to first get to know each other better before making such an important decision. Frustrated, they came to me for premarital counseling—obviously annoyed at their parents' concerns. The first part of counseling was spent testing and evaluating their Marriage Triangle as shown in this book. When we analyzed the results we discovered that she was very talkative and liked to jump in and solve problems "right now!" In their conversations she would often interrupt or speak for him (saying things like, "I know you really agree with me" before he had a chance to reply). She showed little ability to listen. He struggled to express his thoughts, feelings, or wants to her. Their conflict resolution sessions in my office went nowhere—they could not even stay on the topic at hand. Furthermore, the rest of their couple realm looked like this:

- A very brief acquaintanceship (two months) that included much romance, kissing, touching, and so on.

- Dissimilar ideas about working women, children, and birth control. She thought their differences were intriguing. I thought otherwise!

- He had a history of several dating relationships that included much sexual intercourse. Confidentially, she told me she worried that their relationship was becoming too sexual, too fast. She also worried how his sexual relations with former girlfriends would affect his commitment to her after marriage. Would she be able to trust him around other women?

It should be obvious to you by now that this couple's hormones were working overtime, especially his! There were so many red lights in just the couple dimension of the Marriage Triangle that I hardly knew if I would have time before I retired to explore the other two dimensions of the triangle!

As a result of counseling, this couple made some healthy decisions. First, they decided to get to know each other better in other, nonsexual dimensions of their relationship before deciding about marriage. They contracted to proceed sexually at a slower pace and with boundaries both of them could accept. He agreed to talk more openly about his previous dating relationships and how they might affect their future as a couple. They admitted that their dissimilarities needed to be explored more fully and solutions to these differences agreed upon. Finally, they enrolled in a couple communication skills training program at the local community college to learn to communicate more effectively and resolve their differences in a healthier way. I was very proud of them! Their parents experienced great relief, too! Today, they are still working on these goals.

Before going any further, let's do an assessment of your key couple traits. Please complete and score the short tests in Exhibit 5.1.

To get the most out of the book, make sure you've completed the self-report assessment of your couple traits before reading further. At the end of this chapter I will instruct you on what your scores mean and how to use them to improve your chances of being happily married. But first, let's look at your communication skills in more depth. Since communication and conflict resolution skills are more objectively measured by observation rather than self-reporting, I would like you to examine your communication skills by completing an informative exercise called the Couple Communication Assessment.

𝒮 Couple Communication Assessment

This exercise will help you identify your positive and negative couple communication skills and styles. First, prepare an audiotape cassette deck ahead of time so you can record the conversation you will have. Be sure to first test the volume control on the record mode so you can hear each other during the playback. Sit together in a quiet place. Set the recorder between you to get the best recording while talking. Now, decide on a topic or issue on which the two of you disagree. Examples include vacation choices, wedding plans, career plans, relocating, how many children to

The following represent important values and attitudes. Rate how much you and your partner agree with each other about the following statements. For example, if you agree with each other 100 percent of the time, you should circle "We Strongly Agree." If you agree with each other 50 percent of the time, you should circle "We Neither Agree nor Disagree."

Note that this assessment measures your agreement with each other and not with the statements themselves; if you both regard an assertion as equally untrue for you, you would still circle "We Strongly Agree."

Circle your responses to the right of each item.

	We Strongly Disagree	We Disagree	We Neither Agree Nor Disagree	We Agree	We Agree Strongly

Importance of Marriage

How much do you and your partner agree with each other that . . .

1. Being married is the first or second most important thing in life.	1	2	3	4	5
2. Divorce is not an option.	1	2	3	4	5
3. Marriage involves a covenant with God, not just a legal contract recognized by the law.	1	2	3	4	5

Sum your responses to items 1–3 and write your score here: _____

Gender-Based Roles

How much do you and your partner agree with each other that . . .

4. A husband should help out some with housework, but a wife should organize what needs to be done and when.	1	2	3	4	5
5. Mothers have more natural ability than fathers in relating to infants and toddlers.	1	2	3	4	5

Exhibit 5.1. Assessing Couple Traits

Note: Items 63–74 used with permission of C. E. Rusbult and the American Psychological Association.[1]

Circle your responses to the right of each item.

	We Strongly Disagree	We Disagree	We Neither Agree Nor Disagree	We Agree	We Agree Strongly
6. If a husband and wife disagree about something important, the wife should give in to her husband because he is the main leader of the family.	1	2	3	4	5

Sum your responses to items 4–6 and write your score here: _____

Working Wife

How much do you and your partner agree with each other that . . .

	We Strongly Disagree	We Disagree	We Neither Agree Nor Disagree	We Agree	We Agree Strongly
7. It would be acceptable for the husband to stay home to care for young children while the wife earns the paycheck.	1	2	3	4	5
8. The husband's and children's needs should come before a job or career for a wife.	1	2	3	4	5
9. A mother should feel free to pursue a career or job even when there are preschool children in the home.	1	2	3	4	5

Reverse-score item 8 (see Exhibit 3.1 for directions), then sum your responses to items 7–9 and write your score here: _____

Importance of Material Wealth

How much do you and your partner agree with each other that . . .

	We Strongly Disagree	We Disagree	We Neither Agree Nor Disagree	We Agree	We Agree Strongly
10. Money may not buy happiness in a family, but it sure doesn't hurt.	1	2	3	4	5
11. It is important that the family has the finer things in life.	1	2	3	4	5

Exhibit 5.1. *Continued*

Circle your responses to the right of each item.

	We Strongly Disagree	We Disagree	We Neither Agree Nor Disagree	We Agree	We Agree Strongly
12. It is important to earn an income that makes the family financially well off.	1	2	3	4	5

Sum your responses to items 10–12 and write your score here: _____

Autonomy

How much do you and your partner agree with each other that . . .

13. It creates problems for spouses if they go for a few days without spending much time together as a couple.	1	2	3	4	5
14. In a marriage, having time alone is more important than togetherness.	1	2	3	4	5
15. Married couples do not need to share many recreational interests or hobbies with each other.	1	2	3	4	5

Reverse-score item 13, then sum your responses to items 13–15 and write your score here: _____

Marital Sex

How much do you and your partner agree with each other that . . .

16. Sexual intercourse is the most bonding experience you can have in marriage.	1	2	3	4	5
17. Sexual intercourse in marriage is as much a duty as a source of personal pleasure.	1	2	3	4	5
18. Sexual intercourse in marriage is a key to marital satisfaction.	1	2	3	4	5

Reverse-score item 17, then sum your responses to items 16–18 and write your score here: _____

Exhibit 5.1. *Continued*

Circle your responses to the right of each item.

	We Strongly Disagree	We Disagree	We Neither Agree Nor Disagree	We Agree	We Agree Strongly

19. I desire to have sexual intercourse with my spouse about (write answer here:) _____ times per month.

20. My partner desires to have sexual intercourse with me about (write answer here:) _____ times per month.

Family Planning

How much do you and your partner agree with each other that . . .

	We Strongly Disagree	We Disagree	We Neither Agree Nor Disagree	We Agree	We Agree Strongly
21. Using artificial or chemical birth control methods (the pill, spermicide, condom, and so on) is acceptable in marriage.	1	2	3	4	5
22. Permanent birth control through surgical operation for either husband or wife is acceptable if my spouse and I decide to have no more children.	1	2	3	4	5
23. A couple should delay having children until other important issues are worked out first.	1	2	3	4	5

Sum your responses to items 21–23 and write your score here: _____

24. I prefer to have (write answer here:) _____ children during my lifetime.

25. My partner prefers to have (write answer here:) _____ children during his or her lifetime.

Exhibit 5.1. *Continued*

Circle your responses to the right of each item.

	We Strongly Disagree	We Disagree	We Neither Agree Nor Disagree	We Agree	We Agree Strongly

Couple Boundaries

How much do you and your partner agree with each other that . . .

26. Sharing my feelings and concerns about our relationship with our family members or friends is OK.	1	2	3	4	5
27. Seeking help and advice from a professional counselor or clergy person for problems we have in our relationship is OK.	1	2	3	4	5
28. Keeping our relationship problems just between the two of us is best.	1	2	3	4	5

Reverse-score item 28, then sum your responses to items 26–28 and write your score here: _____

Importance of Religion

How much do you and your partner agree with each other that . . .

29. Spirituality is an important part of life.	1	2	3	4	5
30. Prayer is important.	1	2	3	4	5
31. Some doctrines or practices of your church (or religious body) are hard for you to accept.	1	2	3	4	5

Reverse-score item 31, then sum your responses to items 29–31 and write your score here: _____

Exhibit 5.1. *Continued*

Circle your responses:

	Not Similar	Somewhat Similar	Similar

Background Similarity

How similar are you and your partner on these background characteristics?

	Not Similar	Somewhat Similar	Similar
32. Race (Caucasian, African American, Asian American, and so on)	0	1	2
33. Religion	0	1	2
34. Socioeconomic background (middle class, lower class, and so on)	0	1	2
35. Education level	0	1	2
36. Intelligence	0	1	2
37. Age	0	1	2
38. All of the above considered together	0	1	2

Acquaintanceship

39. Approximately how many months have you and your partner known each other? (Write answer here:) _____

40. Approximately how many months will it be from now until you and your partner get married? (Write answer here:) _____

Circle your responses:

	Strongly Disagree	Disagree	Undecided	Agree	Strongly Agree
41. I know most of my partner's life goals.	1	2	3	4	5
42. I know how my partner feels about growing up in his or her family.	1	2	3	4	5

Exhibit 5.1. *Continued*

Circle your responses:

	Strongly Disagree	Disagree	Undecided	Agree	Strongly Agree
43. I know the life stressors that my partner is currently experiencing.	1	2	3	4	5

Sum your responses to items 41–43 and write your score here: _____

Living Together

44. Are you currently or have you in the past lived together with your current partner for the primary purpose of sexual intimacy? (Circle your response here:) Yes   No

45. Have you lived together primarily for the purpose of finding out whether you as a couple will get along? (Circle your response here:) Yes   No

46. Are you living together now and both of you plan to marry each other? (Circle your response here:) Yes   No

47. With how many other opposite-sex partners have you lived with in the past for the purpose of sexual intimacy or seeing if you will get along? (Write number here:) _____

Premarital Sex and Pregnancy

48. In how many previous relationships have you engaged in premarital sexual intercourse? (Write number here:) _____

49. In some relationships children are present premaritally. Which statement best describes your current situation? (Circle your answer below.)

   A: There is a pregnancy and the child will be born before marriage.

   B: There is a pregnancy and the child will be born after marriage.

   C: There is a pregnancy that will be terminated.

   D: There is a pregnancy that will result in adoption.

   E: We currently have one or more children from this or a previous relationship.

   F: None of the above apply to us.

Exhibit 5.1. *Continued*

50. About how many times have you and your current partner had premarital sex? (Write your response here:) _____

Communication and Conflict Resolution Skills

The following section deals with your communication and conflict resolution skills. Mark your response to each item using the response choices below.

Circle your responses:

	Strongly Disagree	Disagree	Undecided	Agree	Strongly Agree

Empathic Communication

51. In most matters, I understand what my partner is saying.	1	2	3	4	5
52. I understand my partner's feelings.	1	2	3	4	5
53. I am able to listen to my partner in an understanding way.	1	2	3	4	5

Sum your responses to items 51–53 and write your score here: _____

Clear Sending

54. When I talk to my partner, I can say what I want in a clear manner.	1	2	3	4	5
55. I struggle to find words to express myself to my partner.	1	2	3	4	5
56. I discuss my personal problems with my partner.	1	2	3	4	5

First reverse-score item 55, then sum your responses to items 54–56 and write your score here: _____

Partner's Empathic Communication

57. In most matters, my partner understands what I am trying to say.	1	2	3	4	5

Exhibit 5.1. *Continued*

Circle your responses:

	Strongly Disagree	Disagree	Undecided	Agree	Strongly Agree
58. My partner understands my feelings.	1	2	3	4	5
59. My partner is able to listen to me in an understanding way.	1	2	3	4	5

Sum your responses to items 57–59 and write your score here: _____

Partner's Clear Sending

	Strongly Disagree	Disagree	Undecided	Agree	Strongly Agree
60. My partner can say what he or she wants to say in a clear manner.	1	2	3	4	5
61. My partner struggles to find words to express himself or herself to me.	1	2	3	4	5
62. My partner discusses his or her personal problems with me.	1	2	3	4	5

Reverse-score item 61, then sum your responses to items 60–62 and write your score here: _____

Conflict Resolution Responses

The following items refer to how you and your partner resolve problems or conflict in your relationship. Read each item and circle your responses to the right.

Circle your responses:

	We Never Do This	We Seldom Do This	We Sometimes Do This	We Frequently Do This	We Always Do This

Exit Responses

	We Never Do This	We Seldom Do This	We Sometimes Do This	We Frequently Do This	We Always Do This
63. When I'm unhappy with my partner, I consider breaking up.	1	2	3	4	5

Exhibit 5.1. *Continued*

Circle your responses:

	We Never Do This	We Seldom Do This	We Sometimes Do This	We Frequently Do This	We Always Do This
64. When I'm irritated with my partner, I think about ending our relationship.	1	2	3	4	5
65. When I'm dissatisfied with our relationship, I consider dating other people.	1	2	3	4	5

Sum your responses to items 63–65 and write your score here: _____

Voice Response

	We Never Do This	We Seldom Do This	We Sometimes Do This	We Frequently Do This	We Always Do This
66. When my partner says or does things I don't like, I talk to him or her about what's upsetting me.	1	2	3	4	5
67. When things aren't going well between us, I suggest changing things in the relationship in order to solve the problem.	1	2	3	4	5
68. When my partner and I are angry with one another, I suggest a compromise.	1	2	3	4	5

Sum your responses to items 66–68 and write your score here: _____

Loyalty Responses

	We Never Do This	We Seldom Do This	We Sometimes Do This	We Frequently Do This	We Always Do This
69. When we have problems in our relationship, I patiently wait for things to improve.	1	2	3	4	5
70. When there are things about my partner that I don't like, I accept his or her faults and weaknesses and don't try to change him or her.	1	2	3	4	5
71. When my partner is inconsiderate, I give him or her the benefit of the doubt and forget about it.	1	2	3	4	5

Sum your responses to items 69–71 and write your score here: _____

Exhibit 5.1. *Continued*

Circle your responses:

	We Never Do This	We Seldom Do This	We Sometimes Do This	We Frequently Do This	We Always Do This
Neglect Responses					
72. When my partner and I have problems, I refuse to talk to him or her about it.	1	2	3	4	5
73. When I'm really bothered about something my partner has done, I criticize him or her for things that are unrelated to the real problem.	1	2	3	4	5
74. When I'm upset with my partner, I ignore him or her for a while.	1	2	3	4	5

Sum your responses to items 72–74 and write your score here: _____

Exhibit 5.1. *Continued*

have, birth control, budgeting money, or anything else that you genuinely care about. (Please don't have a fight while trying to decide!) Turn on the recorder and begin discussing the topic. Continue the discussion for about three minutes. Then stop the recording.

To score this behavioral measure of your communication and conflict resolution skills, first rewind the tape to the beginning of your conversation. Each of you should score yourself, not your partner, on each of the communication behaviors listed in Exhibit 5.2. As you play the tape, stop after each short segment of interaction and score your skills. This will require that you listen to small segments of the tape at a time until you have listened to the entire conversation. Don't feel overwhelmed! This is only a three-minute interaction. Even though it is a short conversation, you will learn much about your communication and conflict resolution skills.

This communication exercise completes your assessment of your couple traits. As promised earlier, at the end of the chapter I will show you how to use your scores and responses to determine your strengths and areas for improvement in your couple realm. But first, let's look carefully at the relationship between couple traits and your later marital satisfaction.

✊ The Importance of Similarities

Similarities have long been recognized as promoting later marital satisfaction—this is intuitive to most couples. When you are similar, you know what to expect from each other, whereas differences require negotiation and compromise.[2] Thus similarities are assets on your "marital balance sheet" and differences are liabilities.

What are the most important similarities you and your partner should consider before marrying? Our research suggests that agreements with each other in these areas are most predictive of later marital satisfaction:

1. *The importance of marriage.* Is marriage most important to you in your life or does it fall behind your career or hobbies? Is it so important that you would never consider divorce if you were having marital problems (other than abuse, addiction, or other things that would make it actively dangerous to stay in the marriage)?

Mark how many times each of you did each of the following:

Record the number of times: Her   Him

Positive Speaking Skills:

   1. I expressed a thought, or feeling, or intention in a respectful way. _____ _____

   2. I made positive suggestions to resolve our disagreement.   _____ _____

Add up the number of times each of you used each of the
positive speaking skills in items 1 and 2 and write your totals here: _____ _____

Negative Speaking Skills:

   3. I kept my thoughts, feelings, or intentions to myself and said little. _____ _____

   4. I made no suggestions or negative suggestions to resolve our
      disagreement.   _____ _____

   5. I tried to force my solution to the problem on my partner.   _____ _____

Add up the number of times each of you used each of the negative
speaking skills in items 3, 4, and 5 and write your totals here: _____ _____

Positive Listening Skills:

   6. I asked my partner for information on his or her opinion.   _____ _____

   7. I responded to my partner's comments or solutions to the
      problem in a tolerant, caring way.   _____ _____

Add up the number of times each of you used each of the positive
listening skills in items 6 and 7 and write your totals here: _____ _____

Negative Listening Skills:

   8. I was intolerant or judgmental about my partner's point of view. _____ _____

   9. I interrupted my partner when he or she was speaking.   _____ _____

Add up the number of times each of you used each of the negative
listening skills in items 8 and 9 and write your totals here: _____ _____

Exhibit 5.2. Scoring Sheet for Couple Communication Assessment[3]

Nonverbal Behaviors:

The next group of items ask each of you to rate your nonverbal behaviors. Read each item and respond by using one of the responses to the right of each item. Mark an "X" over the number for his response and circle the number for her response.

	Strongly Disagree	Disagree	Undecided	Agree	Strongly Agree

Positive Behaviors:

	Strongly Disagree	Disagree	Undecided	Agree	Strongly Agree
10. I maintained direct eye contact.	1	2	3	4	5
11. I nodded my head or said "Uh-huh" occasionally to show my partner I was listening.	1	2	3	4	5

Negative Behaviors:

	Strongly Disagree	Disagree	Undecided	Agree	Strongly Agree
12. I slouched back in my chair most of the time while listening.	1	2	3	4	5
13. My arms or legs were crossed most of the time.	1	2	3	4	5

The next group of items ask each of you to rate the overall conversation. Read each item and respond by using one of the responses to the right of each item. Mark an "X" over the number for his response and circle the number for her response.

	Strongly Disagree	Disagree	Undecided	Agree	Strongly Agree
14. This conversation fostered our relationship.	1	2	3	4	5
15. As a couple we stayed with one issue, not straying to other issues.	1	2	3	4	5
16. Each of us had about equal speaking time.	1	2	3	4	5

Exhibit 5.2. *Continued*

2. *Gender roles in marriage.* Do you have more traditional or more egalitarian attitudes about husband and wife roles? More important, are your role expectations similar or different from your partner's? Dissimilarities on this dimensions can lead to frustrating and annoying arguments over who is supposed to do what in marriage.

3. *Careers.* Since most wives want or need to work sometime after marriage and husbands increasingly want to be more involved in raising their children, this is an important similarity for you to consider. This involves answering the questions of who works, when, for how many hours per week, and so on. That discussion then leads into a discussion of who cares for the children, when, for how long, and so on.

4. *Importance of material wealth.* If the two of you disagree on the importance of money in your relationship it will be like a pebble in your marital shoe—constantly rubbing against the skin of your relationship and irritating both of you. Conflict over money is a very common cause of marital dissatisfaction. Often the conflict is not about how to budget money (a skill) but rather about the relative importance of money and material things to each of you.

5. *Autonomy.* Autonomy refers to your own individuality and privacy in marriage. Disagreements over how much separateness versus togetherness you should have in your relationship are especially common early in marriage when you and your partner are working out your approach to sharing a life. I once heard a wife resentfully say to her husband, "I didn't marry you to be alone!" This statement reflected her greater need for togetherness compared to his. It is not bad to want time and space alone after marriage. That's not the issue. The issue is how different or similar you are in your needs for togetherness versus separateness. The more similar you are in this need, the less friction in your marriage.

6. *Marital sex.* The place of sexual intercourse in marriage is another important topic for you to discuss before marriage. Not only is the importance of sex in marriage essential to discuss, expectations about the frequency of intercourse are good to discuss before going on your honeymoon! In addition, under what circumstances do the two of you agree that you should avoid having intercourse (for example, menstruation, physical illness, stress, fatigue, pregnancy, or whatever)? During those times, how can you express yourselves sexually in

a comfortable and mutually satisfying manner (for example, kissing, hugging, holding hands)? Don't despair if you disagree somewhat on the importance of sex in marriage—that is common. But if the difference is large or you feel unable to resolve your differences on this subject, *go slow!!* A deeper and longer discussion of this subject may be necessary—and it may also be useful to involve a more objective third party in the discussion. Remember what I tell my students: "If sex is good in marriage, it is good; if it is bad, it is *really* bad!"

Remember, too, the importance of a good sex education before marriage. Some experts have estimated that most sexual problems in marriage can be avoided by simply understanding normal human sexual behavior and gender differences in sexual needs and behaviors.

7. *Family planning.* After your discussion of the importance of sex and its frequency in marriage, you should discuss your attitudes about family planning and your preferred methods of birth control. It is especially important to discuss your attitudes on abortion. This will make the transition into marriage much easier for you, help avoid unplanned or unwanted pregnancies, and reduce the trauma related to deciding what to do with such pregnancies. It will also make the honeymoon go more smoothly! You also need to discuss how many children you want and how far apart they will be spaced. Compromise may be necessary if desires differ greatly.

8. *Couple boundaries.* I will never forget a marriage counseling case I recently had where the wife exclaimed in horror and disgust: "He even told his parents about our problems! I'll bet the whole family knows about us now! I'm so ashamed!" There are advantages and disadvantages to breaching the marriage boundary this way. An advantage is that you will be likely to get some form of encouragement to work through your marital problems. Your family may even have some good ideas on how to solve your problems. A disadvantage, of course, is that you may cause these loved ones to worry and fret about the future of your marriage and perhaps interfere inappropriately when they should not. Plus there is the embarrassment of feeling like you are failing in life's most important role—husband or wife. Most important, how similar are your attitudes about boundaries? If you fail to discuss this topic now, you will regret it later when you make a discovery such as the wife did in this example.

9. *Importance of religion.* Many people consider their religious beliefs and practices to be their most important life values. Their religious beliefs define what life, marriage, and family mean. They provide meaning to life and a direction. They provide a set of behavior standards (for example, forgiveness is good). Hence, similarity of religion or beliefs is very important to your future marital satisfaction. Many others have lost touch with religious values entirely, and conduct their lives according to more or less clearly formed ethical principles. It is entirely possible to be in someone's company fairly often over a period of months without noticing the place of religion in their life—but it is not possible to conduct a marriage on that basis. Although people from both groups—religious and nonreligious—tend to believe that everyone else feels as they do, or would do so if they only gave the issues a few minutes' thought, differences in this area are in fact very deeply held and apt to spill over into many aspects of family life.

10. *Background similarity.* The chances of your marital satisfaction are greater if you marry someone whose background characteristics are similar to yours. These characteristics include race, religion, socioeconomic status, education level, intelligence, and age. People usually marry someone with a similar background because they tend to prefer people who are like them and feel uncomfortable around those who are different. People who are similar on these dimensions share similar topics to talk about, their values are similar, and their interests overlap. They feel a sense of compatibility early. In addition, if you marry someone who is very different from you on these factors, you will probably meet with overt or subtle disapproval from family and friends. And as noted earlier, parents' and friends' disapproval can cause much distress in marriage. As with dissimilarity of values and attitudes, dissimilarity of backgrounds requires partners to negotiate and compromise more often than partners who are similar. Each couple must decide for themselves how much compromising or accepting of differences they can tolerate in their relationship. Of course, there are many happy, stable marriages between people who have come from different religions, racial or ethnic backgrounds, or classes. Social scientists need to study these couples more intensely to discover how they manage their differences in ways that enhance marital satisfaction.

In summary, there are ten important similarities to assess in your relationship when considering marriage:

- Importance of marriage
- Gender role expectations
- Workforce participation
- Importance of material wealth
- Autonomy
- Importance of marital sex
- Family planning ideas
- Couple boundaries
- Importance of religion
- Backgrounds

These are not listed in order of importance—researchers have not distinguished yet which similarities are most important in marriage and which are least important. All of them should be considered as important discussion topics for you and your partner. My advice to you is simple: *maximize your similarities whenever possible.* In areas where are you dissimilar, thoroughly discuss the issue and then decide either to accept each other's differences or to come to a compromise on how such differences will be managed in your marriage.

Let me give you an example of how a couple compromised on some important differences. Sol (twenty-four) and Dena (twenty-three) were about to get engaged but felt a strong need to first look closely at two values where they differed greatly: the importance of material wealth and couple boundaries. Their values looked like this:

- *Sol:*
  Material wealth is one of my highest life priorities.
  Sharing marital problems with family members is a valid way to solve them.

- *Dena:*
  Material wealth is not a life priority; making ends meet is the goal.
  Couple privacy is essential—we must be able to resolve our problems independently.

I suggested that they first discuss their different values so each person really understood the other. I emphasized, "Seek to understand first!" Then they discussed these options: persuading my partner to believe what I do, accepting our differences and learning to adapt to each other in mutually satisfying ways, or compromising on issues where these differences would cause tension. Since they were so strong in their beliefs on these two issues, they dismissed persuading each other as a viable option. (I agreed with them wholeheartedly on this—persuasion seldom works!) Accepting their differences and learning to live with them did not seem possible. So, they pursued the third option—compromising. Here's what they came up with through a long discussion and give-and-take:

First, they would work hard together to earn enough money to meet both their basic needs (for example food, clothes, housing, autos, and so on), and just a few of the most important "higher needs"—defined as an expensive vacation every other year, leasing a new car every three years, and paying extra toward their home mortgage so it could be paid off earlier. Second, they agreed to keep their marital problems to themselves and work out problems alone. If this strategy failed, they agreed to go to Sol's father in private and ask for his advice (he was the most respected and trusted family member on both sides). Both agreed to not share their problems with any other family members or friends. Hence, Dena got a good measure of the privacy she valued and Sol received the social support he needed.

Such compromises are frequently necessary even if the two of you feel you are very similar. No doubt, after marriage you will find some values and attitudes that are dissimilar. Don't despair—compromise is possible! By the way, if you cultivate the personality trait described earlier as flexibility, compromises will come easier.

Now let me share an example of acceptance of values differences. Martin (twenty-eight) and Sheryl (twenty-six) had very dissimilar views on autonomy. He preferred lots of time alone, in his study or at the library, to read, meditate, and write. Sheryl valued togetherness—preferring to do just about anything *with* Martin rather than without him. Having him with her to share an experience made the occasion much more meaningful to her. After much discussion of their difference they admitted to each other that a compromise was not possible—it seemed that one of them would always end up upset when they tried compromising. So, they "agreed to disagree" and accept each other's unique needs. In doing so Martin accepted the idea that sometimes Sheryl could ask a friend rather than him to go to a movie with her. She accepted that he often needed his space and learned not to interpret his need to be alone as a rejection of her (which she used to do). This acceptance of autonomy differences worked for Sheryl and Martin—but acceptance may not work for you as a couple. You need to decide whether compromise or acceptance works best for you for each of the ten important similarities.

The Importance of Acquaintanceship

I define *acquaintanceship* as a combination of how well you know your partner (depth of knowledge) and how long you've known your partner (breadth of experiences) before marriage. The relationship between acquaintanceship and later marital satisfaction is simple: the longer and better you know someone before marriage, the greater the likelihood of marital satisfaction. This is because the longer you become acquainted with someone before marriage—usually—the better you know them, understand them, and understand your couple strengths and weaknesses. Researchers are increasingly emphasizing that a major linchpin of a lasting marriage is friendship. Couples whose marriages last know each other on many levels. For example, each person knows much about the other's likes, dislikes, personality quirks, hopes, and dreams.[4]

Much of this friendship should develop before marriage. That takes time. Some argue that it's how deeply you know someone that's important, not how long you have known them. I argue that part of the quality (depth) of your acquaintance is dependent on the quantity of time you have spent together. An example helps illustrate this point.

A young woman I was counseling to go slow in her progress toward marriage argued, "But, Dr. Larson, even though we have only known each other for a month we have spent many hours sharing our lifes' goals, dreams, likes, and dislikes. I feel like I've known him for two years already! So why wait any longer to get serious about this relationship? We want to get engaged." I congratulated her for getting to know him on a deeper level but warned her that continuing to date and get to know him even better was the wisest thing to do. I emphasized that it is easy to see just your compatibilities in the first stages of a relationship—that's part of romantic love. But friendship takes much longer to develop. It takes shared experiences over time. I stressed that knowing him for a longer period would allow her to see other sides of him—his personal quirks, how he responds in a crisis, how he handles stress, how he relates to his family, how he deals with important dates like her birthday, how the two of them handle conflict, and so on and on. All this cannot be learned in a few months. She countered with a story of how she had recently received divine inspiration that this was the right guy to marry. I respectfully asked her if he, too, had received such inspiration (which would make it more likely that the inspiration was not, in fact, perspiration). And, even so, would the source of this inspiration (in her case, God) disagree with their getting better acquainted before marriage? "Gee, I guess not," she said.

Eight months later she thanked me for my advice and told me that she and her boyfriend had broken up. Why? Over time she discovered that he had a gambling addiction he was ashamed of and hadn't wanted to admit to her earlier in the relationship. He admitted that he had not solved this problem yet. That explained why he often complained of being broke even though he was working two jobs. His addiction had resulted in his frequently borrowing money from her. At the end of their relationship he owed her $6,000! If she had not let time pass and gotten to know him better, she might have jumped into a marriage with an addict and not known it until several months later.

So acquaintanceship provides you with many advantages—including giving you the opportunity to become more aware of differences, to experience conflicts, and to help screen out incompatible partners. Successful conflict resolution gives you the confidence that you can deal effectively with problems after marriage, too. Finally, the longer you become acquainted, the better you will know his family of origin and the better the chances that they will accept and approve of your marriage.

Now, I know what you're thinking! How long is long enough to know each other before marriage? Research cannot answer this question—we simply do not know the minimum length of time partners should know each other before marriage to maximize their chances of being happily married. In the United States, however, we know about how long most couples know each other before marriage. The median length of acquaintance from first meeting to marriage is about two years and the median length of engagement is about eleven months.[5] These may seem like long periods of time but remember, for some couples those times are partially spent living together before marriage. My advice to you is to get acquainted for *at least one year* before marriage (this may or may not include an engagement period). This will give you a chance to observe your partner through all the seasons of the year, during school and summer vacations (as applicable) and also give you time to get to know your partner's family better (many individuals take their partner home to meet the folks during holidays). One year gives most couples the minimum time period necessary to answer many of the important questions discussed in this chapter about their partner and their relationship.

I also advise you to complete an important ritual before deciding on an engagement: Go camping together overnight (taking two tents if you prefer not to share sleeping quarters). Take few provisions or comforts of home with you. There's nothing quite like the great outdoors to bring out awful qualities in your partner that you otherwise might never see! That's because camping puts stress on people—it pulls them out of their comfort zone. For example, when camping you probably wind up eating partially cooked food with bugs in it and usually in the dark. You both smell like campfire smoke. You get to see what each other looks like in the morning with uncombed hair and unwashed face—and oh, that breath! You may learn that he is unsympathetic and rude when you cry out in the night that there's a bear in the camp, and just yells, "Oh, shut up and go back to sleep!" Some protector of the home he will make! You may learn that she laughs when you slip in the mud, and reaches for the camera instead of the first aid kit. Some support and helpmate you've got here! And last but not least, your partner may expect *you* to take down the tents and pack the car!

More seriously, try the camping experience or some other challenging adventure (for example, white-water rafting) before you get engaged, to see how well you and your partner react to stress and crises. Do you work together as a team? Or are you at each other's throats?

Let me end this section with a quote from therapist Neil Warren: "When a couple is ready to decide on something as all encompassing as marriage after only a few weeks or months of dating, I assume their decision is long on fantasy and short on reality."[6]

🕉 Living Together

Many people believe that living together (cohabitation) before marriage is a good idea because it gives a couple a chance to test their compatibility. The hope is that cohabitation will serve as kind of a trial marriage. Some individuals cohabit with several people over their lifetime, trying to find the right one. We call these people "serial cohabitors."

Unfortunately, however, such people actually *increase* their chances for divorce![7] One of the most consistent research findings in the mate selection literature is that "no positive contribution of cohabitation to marriage has ever been found."[8] Why is this so? There are several reasons. First, people willing to live together are more unconventional than others and tend to be less committed to marriage as an institution. These two factors make it easier for them to leave a marriage later if it becomes unsatisfying. Second, there is evidence that cohabitors value autonomy more than noncohabitors, and marriage involves less autonomy for both partners than living together. Finally, cohabitors are more likely than noncohabitors to accept divorce; their enthusiasm for marriage and childbearing tends to dwindle the longer they live together.[9]

Serial cohabitation is the biggest problem. If you or your partner have previously lived with someone else, the relationship between living together and later divorce may be especially strong. This is probably due to the experience of dissolving a cohabiting relationship generating a greater willingness to dissolve later relationships. These individuals may also have a relatively low tolerance for unhappiness in a relationship.

On the other hand, cohabitation when both people plan to marry each other as a prelude to marriage during the engagement period is different from serial cohabitation or living together as an experiment, to see if it will work. The negative effects of this type of cohabitation on a subsequent marriage appear to be less.

In summary, living together will not increase your chances of being happily married and may actually decrease your chances. So if you currently live together or plan to live together ask yourselves these important questions: What are your major reasons for living together? How is living together related to your decision to get married? For example, is living together a substitute for marriage? Is it to see if you are well-matched? Is it a trial marriage? How will living together strengthen or weaken your commitment to this relationship? How is it related to your need for autonomy? How is it related to your attitude about divorce? What will be the likely reaction of your parents, relatives, and friends if you live together?

As you can tell by these questions, I believe you should not make this decision casually.

🎱 Premarital Sex and Pregnancy

When we were going out I worried that her sexual experiences with other men before we met might cause us a problem later if we got married. But she reassured me that *I* was different from all those other men. But sure enough, after only two years of marriage and the birth of our son she was going out on me!

—Russell (twenty-five), separated from his wife

When we found out I was pregnant the rest didn't really matter. Now we felt we just *had* to get married! The trick was, how to hide it from our parents long enough to get the job done. Well, we couldn't and they were very disappointed in us. It was sad, too, because up to that point I wasn't even sure I wanted to marry Ron.

—Aleese (twenty), college student and mother

These are two sad stories about the potential effects of premarital sexual intercourse and pregnancy on later marital satisfaction. Research shows that sexual relations with multiple partners before marriage is a predictor of later divorce, especially for women.[10] There are several explanations for this. First, waiting until you are married before having sexual intercourse increases your respect for marriage as an institution. Marriage is, then, "more special." Second, remaining a virgin until marriage is called a traditional view by sociologists—and a traditional view of marriage is related to higher marital satisfaction for most couples.[11]

By a traditional view of marriage, I mean marriage is seen as a one-time, permanent relationship that a person commits to totally with an expectation of sexual fidelity. In contrast, those who have premarital sex are more likely than virgins to have more liberal attitudes about marriage, have less commitment to marriage, and more liberal attitudes about divorce. "Women who engage in premarital sex may have done so because they valued personal fulfillment and satisfaction more than traditional expectations of chastity. If they felt less constrained by traditional norms prior to marriage, they may also feel less constrained by norms about the permanence of marriage."[12]

Third, those engaging in premarital sex may mistake the physical intimacy of sex for love and emotional compatibility prior to marriage. Fourth, engaging in premarital sex may violate one's moral standards and lead to chronic guilt and/or church censure. Fifth, sexual experiences with other partners before marriage may encourage individuals to have unrealistically high expectations for fulfillment within marriage and thus increase their chances for disappointment.[13] And, sixth, liberal sexual behavior before marriage increases the chances of extramarital sex in marriage.[14]

In summary, there are several ways that premarital sex may lead to later marital dissatisfaction. Thus if you have had sexual intercourse with others or are having sexual intercourse with your current partner, you should examine your values and attitudes about marriage and sex to see if they fit any of those discussed here. Then ask yourself these important questions: How is your attitude about premarital sex related to your attitude about marriage in general? Commitment? Divorce? How is your attitude about premarital sex related to your attitude about extramarital sex? How is sex different from love? How has premarital sex affected you morally? How will it affect your standing in your church? How will premarital sex be an asset for you in your marriage?

The obvious evidence of premarital sex is pregnancy! What will a premarital pregnancy do for your chances of being happily married? Simply, it will lower your chances. This is due to many factors:[15]

- Young age at marriage. Many premarital pregnancies occur among young adults under the age of twenty.

- Disagreement on how to deal with the pregnancy. For example, one partner may favor keeping the child while the other favors adoption or abortion. In the end, who makes the decision? And how will the decision affect your future marriage if you go against the wishes of your partner? This decision is so important and surrounded by such intense emotions that many couples who face it benefit greatly from counseling with a licensed professional. The decision will have long-term negative or positive effects not only on you but on your marriage. Negative effects are especially common if abortion is chosen because of the seriousness of the act.

- External and internal pressures—from parents or the couple's own guilt feelings—to get married to give the child a married mother and father when, in fact, the couple may not be ready to get married. Thus they may feel pushed into a marriage prematurely.

- An unplanned marriage and parenthood usually interfere with school completion and career preparation, which may later lead to resentment of this marriage and family obligation.

- The cumulative stress associated with marriage and parenthood occurring within months of each other. Either event is stressful enough by itself! You don't want to have to become a spouse and a parent at the same time.

- Negative emotional reactions. Many relationships involving a premarital pregnancy result in one or both partners feeling depressed, angry, resentful, guilty, or just plain stuck. What a poor emotional level on which to start a marriage! Instead, you should approach marriage with happiness, excitement, pride, and self-assurance, and with little pressure.

- The birth of a child close to marriage inhibits a couple from developing compatibility and bonding that must be done in private in the first stage of marriage.

If you are pregnant and considering marriage you should ask yourself these important questions: If there were no pregnancy, would we still get married anyway? Looking at the rest of our Marriage Triangle, how good do our chances of a satisfying marriage look? How do we feel about the decision we have made to deal with pregnancy and how will it affect our marriage? Is our decision to marry based mostly on pleasing others (for example, parents, relatives, or friends)? How will we complete school and career plans while adjusting to parenthood? What negative emotional reactions to the pregnancy do we need to resolve first? How can we plan our marriage and the childbirth so as to lessen the stress on us and our families? If we marry, how will we manage being parents and nurturing our marriage in its infancy? Who can help us with this task? (For example, will grandparents be willing to care for the child periodically to give you privacy to bond?)

The Importance of Communication

Good communication is the key to intimacy in marriage—it is the lifeblood of marital relations.[16] Communication is defined as the ability of partners to send messages clearly, understand each other's messages, and resolve conflicts in a manner that maintains or strengthens the relationship.

Communication involves both skills and attitudes. That is, you must have both good skills and a caring attitude to make a relationship work. Some individuals have good skills but a selfish attitude. This leads to manipulation of their partner. For example, you may listen to your partner with empathy but, in fact, have no intention of considering their point of view when making a decision; their point of view *really* doesn't matter. This shows up after your listening moment, when you say, "I can see going to the conference with me is important to you, but *I* make the decisions around here about how the money is spent, and you're not going!"

Other individuals have a caring attitude but no skills. This results in misunderstandings.[17] Partners of such people complain, "He is the sweetest guy on earth— I know he really loves me. But we constantly miscommunicate when we discuss important things. He can't seem to tell me what he really feels or wants."

So to be an effective communicator your attitude must be kind and loving, and your speaking, listening, and conflict resolution skills must be sharp. I cannot help you with your attitude—that is up to you. Just be aware of its key importance when trying to use communication skills, and remember that you cannot fake it and successfully communicate. Now let's look at the skills you need for a satisfying marriage. They include sending or speaking skills, empathy or understanding skills, and conflict resolution skills.

Sending Skills

One of the keys to building intimacy and resolving conflict in marriage is self-awareness and the ability to express your thoughts and feelings clearly and appropriately in words. Counselors sometimes refer to this skill as *I-messages*. The formula is: "I feel [specific emotion] when you [engage in some specific behavior] because [it has this specific effect on me]. Clear sending also involves expressing your thoughts and wants. Here are some examples of clear sending of feelings, thoughts, and wants:

"I feel frustrated when you pick me up late at night because I'm really tired and it keeps me from getting the rest I need."

"I feel closer to you when you tell me how you feel about our relationship because I need to know."

"I thought you didn't care when you said no so bluntly when I asked you to go to the café with me."

"I think this solution will work best for us because we both get our needs met, not just one of us."

"I want to go to a quiet, peaceful place this weekend because I've had such a hectic week."

"I want us to be closer as a result of these talks."

You can see from these statements how intimacy, closeness, and clarity are engendered in the relationship.

Empathic Listening

The second skill you need to effectively communicate on important topics is empathic listening. Empathy is the ability to stand in someone else's shoes and see the world from their perspective. It is nonjudgmental. It is not interpreting what your partner says but rather reflecting what they have said in a short paraphrase or simply responding with sincere short phrases like, "Uh-huh," "I see," or "Right!" It is a skill to use when your partner is expressing feelings, thoughts, or wants on an important topic. It is not used in everyday, small-talk conversations about the weather, what's up, answering questions, and so on. Here are some examples of using clear sending and empathic listening skills in the same conversation:

HIM: What a day! I'm so tired I could fall down. I did more today than the last three days combined. I can't keep up this pace.

HER: You sound really exhausted!

HIM: I am! If my boss doesn't hire more help for me, we're going to have a shoot-out.

HER: So you may have to have it out with him.

HIM: That's right. When I was hired he told me the job could be done in forty hours a week. But it's taking a lot longer than that. And I'm on salary, so they're getting more of me than I bargained for. It's not fair.

HER: You're not being treated fairly.

HIM: No, and it's got to stop!

HER: Right!

If you were the him here, how would you feel at the end of this short conversation? Understood? Appreciated? Somewhat relieved? Notice that she did not offer advice, act critical (say, "Well, why did you take the job in the first place?") or ignore him. She simply paraphrased how he felt and offered it back to him. It works! After first listening to him, she has earned the right to ask him if he would like some advice. If he says yes, she can make suggestions. The problem in most serious conversations is that we give advice to our partner too early in the interaction. Many times, advice is not only not wanted, but not needed. People can usually come up with their own solutions—they just need to blow off some steam first.

Related speaking skills (for example, speaking in a respectful way) and empathy (for example, asking for a partner's opinion) are discussed next as part of conflict resolution skills. Resolving conflict in healthy ways is one of the single best predictors of marital satisfaction. Hence, your ability to do so is crucial for you to assess before marriage.

Conflict Resolution Skills

Effective conflict resolution involves the use of clear sending and empathic listening skills as described earlier. In addition, the following related skills assist couples in effectively dealing with conflict and at the same time enriching the relationship:[18]

Related Speaking Skills

Using respect when stating your opinion.

Making positive suggestions.

Avoiding forcing your solution on your partner.

Not straying from the topic at hand.

Calming yourself when the disagreement is intense.

Related Listening Skills

Using a caring tone of voice.

Avoiding interrupting.

Asking your partner for his opinion.

Giving your partner equal speaking time.

Maintaining eye contact and an open body position (for example not crossing your arms or fidgeting).

Calming your partner when the disagreement is intense.

Here is an example of how a couple dealt with a conflict in a premarital counseling session in my office. They had learned many of the skills listed in this chapter, partly by observing their parents' good role modeling and partly as a result of participating in a marriage preparation course at their church. The topic they discussed was where to go for their honeymoon. Previous assessment indicated there was still a disagreement or conflict about where to go.

APRIL: I really don't want to go out of the country. We just won't have time. We both have to be back to our jobs by Monday and I don't want to go in tired and cranky. *(Expression of wants.)*

JOHN: So, not being exhausted is important to you. *(Empathic response.)*

APRIL: Yeah.

JOHN: Well, having a great time in an exotic place is more important to me than worrying about what happens after the honeymoon. After all, you only go on one honeymoon in your life. I want to splurge as much as possible.

APRIL: Uh-huh. *(Empathic response.)*

JOHN: Which reminds me, have you withdrawn that money from our savings account that you said you would? *(Straying off topic.)*

APRIL: Before we discuss that, could we please decide where we're going first? *(Respectfully bringing John back on topic.)*

JOHN: OK. I don't want you to go on a trip and dread coming home tired, but at the same time, the more tired you are when you come home, the better time you must have had, right? *(Shows respect for her opinion, then states his own thought.)*

APRIL: I see what you mean. *(Said in a caring tone of voice.)*

JOHN: But seriously, if both of us are not happy with where we go, we might as well not go. *(Avoiding forcing his solution on his partner.)*

APRIL: Right! There must be places that are both exotic and relatively close. You know, tourists come from all over the world to visit our state and see the national parks, mountains, rivers, lakes, and all that. Remember the German and Japanese tourists we saw at Arches last week? *(Making a positive suggestion.)*

JOHN: Yeah, they were interesting. So you think we could honeymoon right here in good ole' Utah? *(Asking partner for her opinion.)*

APRIL: It's a possibility. There are several parks we have never visited. And we can get back home from any of them within half a day. *(States a thought.)*

JOHN: They're convenient, that's for sure. *(Empathic response.)* But you know, I really want to get away—you know—go to the beach or some other romantic place. Is there a beach close enough that we could get back to Utah within one day or less? *(Positive suggestion, suggesting a compromise.)*

APRIL: So maybe we could do the beach thing and still get back rested for work. *(Empathic response.)*

JOHN: Yeah!

APRIL: Let's discuss that idea some more tonight. *(Positive suggestion, willingness to compromise.)*

Later that night April and John decided to go to San Diego, California, for their honeymoon and to schedule the trip so they would be back in Utah early enough to get the rest before work that April desired. For this couple, compromising worked well. When you compromise, each person yields or gives in until together you find a middle ground or devise an alternative solution. Most conflicts in marriage can be negotiated this way.

There are, however, other styles of conflict resolution that couples use. I like Rusbult and Zembrodt's typology of conflict resolution (Figure 5.2), which concisely and scientifically describes these styles.[19]

Let's first define the terms *exit, voice, neglect,* and *loyalty.*

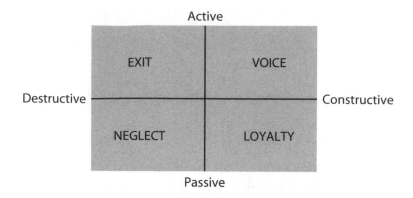

Figure 5.2. Styles of Conflict Resolution

Source: From Rusbult and Zembrodt (1983), p. 277.

Exit refers to separating from one's partner, leaving, moving out, or breaking up.

Voice refers to openly discussing problems, compromising, or changing oneself or one's partner.

Loyalty refers to waiting and hoping that things will improve, praying for improvement, or supporting one's partner.

Neglect refers to ignoring a problem, refusing to discuss it, being critical or insulting, or just letting things fall apart.

One dimension of conflict resolution is *activity–passivity,* which refers to the impact of the response of a partner on the problem being discussed, not to the nature of the behavior itself. For example, storming out of the room is an active behavior but it is passively neglectful in regard to resolving the conflict because it is a refusal to discuss the problem. *Constructiveness–destructiveness* refers to the impact of a partner's response on the relationship, not on the individual. For example, suddenly leaving the house while in conflict may be a constructive way for a partner to handle anger at the moment, but such an exit is clearly destructive to the relationship. Thus, exit (flight) and voice (fight) are active responses, whereas loyalty and neglect are passive in regard to the conflict itself.

As you might guess, couple satisfaction is related to using more constructive responses to conflict than destructive ones. The voice response's advantages are self-evident. The loyalty response is constructive but more passive. This response approach is similar to accepting your partner or at least choosing your fights carefully. It may involve supporting your partner rather than trying to promote change, as well as refraining from criticism, giving the benefit of the doubt, and cultivating forgiveness—all responses that research shows improve marital satisfaction. "Choosing your fights carefully" refers to making a conscious and deliberate choice of which issues in a relationship are worthy of a lengthy discussion, and which ones are not worth the time, effort, and emotional cost to discuss. Examples of the former might be where you honeymoon, how to parent children, and what sorts of housework to share. Examples of the latter might include where to eat tonight, how messy the car gets after your partner uses it, and the annoyance of finding clothes scattered all over the floor.

If you currently use one of the other two types of conflict responses—neglect or exit—chances are high that your relationship is dissatisfying and may not survive. In fact, these destructive ways of responding to conflict are more powerful determinants of your couple functioning than are the constructive responses. This may be because most of us expect our partners to behave well and so we take constructive responses for granted, whereas destructive responses produce far more negative emotions than constructive responses produce positive emotions.[20] Thus it is especially important to eliminate the destructive response styles from your relationship.

An Overview of Couple Factors

Let's review your couple traits that predict future marital satisfaction. These couple traits will inhibit your chances of having a satisfying marriage:

- Being very dissimilar on several of the ten important values described earlier.
- Lack of acquaintanceship before marriage.
- Living together as a trial marriage or having a history of living together with other partners.
- Frequent premarital sexual intercourse with your partner and former partners.
- Premarital pregnancy, especially if you and your partner disagree on dealing with it or you elect abortion.
- Lack of communication and conflict resolution skills.
- Destructive conflict response patterns, that is, exiting or neglect.

Put in a more positive way, you can expect to have *more* marital satisfaction if you cultivate the following traits:

- Similarity on most of the ten important values.
- Solid acquaintanceship before marriage.
- Not living together to test the relationship.
- Little or no premarital sex. (Note: This is not a moralistic statement, but rather a reflection of what research suggests.)
- No premarital pregnancy.
- Good communication and conflict resolution skills.
- Constructive conflict response patterns, that is, voice or loyalty.

Again, social scientists don't know which of these couple factors are most important and which are least important. My opinion is that of these factors, the most important ones are

1. Good communication and conflict resolution skills.
2. Constructive rather than destructive conflict response styles.
3. A long and deep acquaintance.

Remember, the remaining factors are *very* important for you to consider in your assessment of yourself and your relationship before marriage. Just focusing on my top three factors is not enough. Let me finish with an example of this.

Paula (twenty-one) and Tom (twenty-five) were great communicators. Friends admired their skills and would often comment on them. Conflicts were nearly always dealt with constructively. Destructive styles were nonexistent. They had been friends for three and a half years and knew each other well. As a result, they overinterpreted the common trite expression, "With good communication skills, anything is possible in marriage," and got married.

One year later, in marriage counseling, they told me what the rest of their couple traits looked like just before marriage. They came from dissimilar backgrounds and cultures and had totally different ideas about how to divide household chores, the importance of sex and material wealth in their marriage, and autonomy. Recognizing the potential for difficulties, they had decided to live together to see if it would work, that is, if they could iron out their differences. That way they did not have to totally commit to each other just yet. While they were living together, however, she got pregnant and they rushed into marriage soon after.

The best communication skills in the United States did not keep this couple together! They became worn out with the frequent (almost nightly) conflicts over important values and attitude differences in their marriage. They admitted their commitment to the marriage was not great before they married. They felt pressured to marry after discovering the pregnancy. Unfortunately, I could not wave a magic wand and send them back to singles-land to warn them about the other couple predictors of marital dissatisfaction they displayed. They finally called the marriage quits after another six months.

So, please thoughtfully consider *all* the factors described in this chapter before you marry.

🕸 Evaluating Your Own Test Results

Here we go with the most important part of this chapter—evaluating and understanding your couple traits test results. The scoring and interpretation guidelines are divided into the same five major sections as the rest of this chapter, namely

- Similarities
- Acquaintanceship
- Living together
- Premarital sex and pregnancy
- Communication and conflict resolution skills

As in the previous chapters, for many of the short test results, the range of scores possible, the norm score, and significantly high or low scores are listed for you to consider. Fill out the score sheets in Exhibit 5.3 so you have the numbers for the first and last segments in front of you. (The other three were more qualitative, and you will be able to work directly from your answers in Exhibit 5.1.)

Similarity

In the spaces provided, write your sum scores on the specified short tests you completed in Exhibit 5.1. These scores are your assessments of your perceived similarities as a couple on ten important values.

Importance of Marriage Similarity Score (questions 1–3):   _____

       Range: 3–15   Norm Score: .... 13.5   Low: 10.0

Gender-Based Roles Similarity Score (questions 4–6):   _____

Range: 3–15   Norm Score: .... 8.0   Low: 5.0

Working Wife Similarity Score (questions 7–9):   _____

Range: 3–15   Norm Score: .... 10.5   Low: 7.5

Importance of Material Wealth Similarity Score (questions 10–12):   _____

Range: 3–15   Norm Score: .... 9.0   Low: 6.0

Autonomy Similarity Score (questions 13–15):   _____

Range: 3–15   Norm Score: .... 13.0   Low: 10.0

Marital Sex Similarity Score (questions 16–18):   _____

       Range: 3–15   Norm Score: .... 10.0   Low: 7.0

Note: How similar are your answers to questions 19 and 20, and 24 and 25?   _____

Family Planning Similarity Score (questions 21–23):   _____

       Range: 3–15   Norm Score: .... 10.0   Low: 7.0

Couple Boundaries Similarity Score (questions 26–28): _____

       Range: 3–15   Norm Score: .... 10.5   Low: 7.5

Religiosity Similarity Score (questions 29–31): _____

       Range: 3–15   Norm Score: .... 12.0   Low: 9.0

Exhibit 5.3. Couple Traits and Communication Summary

Backgrounds Similarity:

List below the background factors you scored 1 or 2 ("Somewhat Similar" or "Similar") on items 32–38:

1. _____

2. _____

3. _____

4. _____

5. _____

6. _____

7. _____

List the background factors you scored 0 or "Dissimilar" on items 32–38:

1. _____

2. _____

3. _____

4. _____

5. _____

6. _____

7. _____

Communication and Conflict Resolution

Questions 51–62 deal with speaking and listening skills. Write in your sum scores for each short test.

Empathic Communication Score (questions 51–53):   _____

    Range: 3–15   Norm Score: .... 12.0   Low: 9.7

Clear Sending Score (questions 54–56):   _____

    Range: 3–15   Norm Score: .... 12.0   Low: 9.0

Exhibit 5.3. *Continued*

Partner's Empathic Communication Score (questions 57–59): _____

    Range: 3–15   Norm Score: .... 11.8   Low Score: 9.3

Partner's Clear Sending Score (questions 60–62): _____

    Range: 3–15   Norm Score: .... 12.0   Low Score: 9.0

Questions 63–74 deal with conflict resolution response styles. Write in your sum scores for each short test.

Exit Responses Score (questions 63–65): _____

    Range: 3–15   Norm Score: .... 4.2   High Score*: 7.0

(*High scores are significant because they mean you use this style more frequently.)

Voice Responses Score (questions 66–68): _____

    Range: 3–15   Norm Score: .... 10.5   High Score: 13.5

Loyalty Responses Score (questions 69–71): _____

    Range: 3–15   Norm Score: .... 9.3   High Score: 12.3

Neglect Responses Scores (questions 72–74): _____

    Range: 3–15   Norm Score: .... 6.0   High Score: 9.0

Exhibit 5.3. *Continued*

Similarities

Now, let's look at your scores for the similarity items (questions 1-38 in Exhibit 5.3).

First, in what areas are you most similar? *Least* similar? Discuss with your partner how the similarities will be assets in your marriage. Discuss how the dissimilarities will be liabilities in your marriage.

_____

_____

_____

_____

_____

Of the ten similarity factors, for which three is it most important for you as a couple to be similar? How similar are you in these three areas? Why?

_____

_____

_____

_____

_____

Describe how you will deal with your dissimilarities in your marriage. How do you deal with them now?

_____

_____

_____

_____

_____

Acquaintanceship

Now, examine your answers to questions 39–43 in Exhibit 5.1. They are related to how well you know each other.

1. List below those areas in which you know the most about your partner:

   _____

   _____

   _____

   _____

   _____

2. Now, list those areas in which you know the least about your partner:

   _____

   _____

   _____

   _____

   _____

3. By the time you marry, will you have known each other for at least one year as suggested? If not, why?

   _____

   _____

   _____

   _____

   _____

   _____

Based on what you have learned about the importance of acquaintanceship in this chapter and your length and depth of acquaintance, how will your acquaintance be an asset or liability in your marriage? Why? What can you do to become better acquainted? How long do you think you should continue to get to know each other before marrying? Why?

_____

_____

_____

_____

_____

Living Together

Questions 44–47 in Exhibit 5.1 refer to your experiences living together with each other or others. If this section does not apply to you, skip to the next section. If it applies, look at your responses to these questions. Based on what you have learned about living together and later marital satisfaction in this chapter, answer these questions:

What are the major reasons you are living together? How will living together be an asset or liability for your future marriage? How have previous living together relationships affected your current attitude about marriage? How is living together related to your ability to make a lifelong commitment to be married to the same person? How is your attitude about living together similar or different from your attitude about divorce?

_____

_____

_____

_____

_____

Premarital Sex and Pregnancy

Look at your responses to questions 48–50 in Exhibit 5.1. They refer to premarital sex and pregnancy. If you have engaged in premarital sex or there is a pregnancy or a child from a previous relationship, answer these questions based on what you have learned in this chapter:

How will premarital sex in previous relationships be an asset or liability in your marriage? How will sex with your current partner be an asset or liability? How is your attitude about premarital sex related to your attitude about commitment in marriage? Extramarital sex? Divorce? How are sex and love (that is, friendship) related to each other in your relationship? Which is most important to you now? Why? How is sex related to your moral standards? Your standing in your church? How is sex related to how well you have gotten to know your partner in other areas of your relationship (for example, values, life goals, dislikes, fears)? If there is a pregnancy or child, how is this affecting your decision to marry? How will the option you have chosen for dealing with a premarital pregnancy affect your later marriage?

_____

_____

_____

_____

_____

If you disagree on how to deal with the pregnancy, how will that affect your later marital satisfaction? How are you currently dealing with the stressors created by a premarital pregnancy? How has it affected your relationship with your partner? What are your plans for the timing of the birth or other pregnancy options and your marriage?

_____

_____

_____

_____

Communication and Conflict Resolution

There were three parts to your assessment of your current couple communication and conflict resolution skills:

- Speaking and listening skills short tests
- Conflict resolution response styles short tests
- Couple communication behavioral assessment

Exhibit 5.3 provides a summary score sheet for the first two; you can work from Exhibit 5.2 for the third.

Speaking and Listening Skills

Based on your analysis, what are your communication skills strengths? Areas for improvement? What about your partner's strengths and areas for improvement?

_____

_____

_____

_____

_____

How will your skills be an asset or liability to you in your marriage?

_____

_____

_____

_____

_____

What skills do you want to enhance? How will you do that? (See resources in Chapter Eight.)

_____

_____

_____

_____

Conflict Resolution Response Styles

Based on your results and what you have learned in this chapter, answer the following questions:

What is your most frequently used conflict resolution response style? Least frequently used style? How will these styles be assets or liabilities to you in your marriage?

_____

_____

_____

_____

_____

What changes do you need to make in your conflict resolution styles? What is the first step? Where can you get help learning new styles? (See Chapter Eight for resources.)

_____

_____

_____

_____

_____

Couple Communication Behavioral Assessment

So, how did this exercise go? What did you like about it? Dislike? What was the number one insight you gained? Now, let's be more specific.

Based on your results for the verbal skills exercise recorded in Exhibit 5.2, each of you should answer the following questions:

1. What positive verbal behaviors did you do *most* frequently? What negative verbal behaviors did you do *most* frequently? What about your partner?

_____

_____

_____

_____

_____

2. What was your ratio of positive skills to negative skills?

_____

_____

_____

_____

_____

3. How are the positive behaviors assets in your current relationship and future marriage? How are the negative behaviors liabilities?

_____

_____

_____

_____

_____

4. What verbal communication skills do you need to learn that will increase the effectiveness of your conflict resolution? What is the first step? Where can you get help? (See Chapter Eight.)

_____

_____

_____

_____

_____

5. What were your most frequent positive and negative nonverbal behaviors (see items 14–18)? Which behaviors do you need to improve?

_____

_____

_____

_____

_____

6. Look at your responses to items 19–21 and discuss your results. What improvements should be made in these three areas?

_____

_____

_____

_____

_____

Based on your performance on the tape, how do you rate your couple conflict resolution skills? Overall, do you have most of the skills necessary to effectively resolve conflict? How do your answers to these questions affect your decision to marry?

Finally, list your couple traits that will be assets and liabilities to your marriage:

Assets	Liabilities
1. _____	1. _____
2. _____	2. _____
3. _____	3. _____
4. _____	4. _____
5. _____	5. _____
6. _____	6. _____
7. _____	7. _____
8. _____	8. _____
9. _____	9. _____
10. _____	10. _____

Congratulations, again!!! You have now finished assessing the third and last factor in the Marriage Triangle—your couple traits. In the next chapter you will summarize all of your findings and insights from the three dimensions of the triangle and be in a better position to answer some very important questions: Overall, what assets and liabilities do you bring to marriage today? What are your goals and plans for improvement? How does all of this affect your decision to marry or not marry your current partner? Exciting answers await you in Chapter Six!

Your Own Personal Marriage Triangle

Putting the Three Factors Together

This will be the most interesting and important chapter of this book for you because first I will first summarize all you have learned about the three factors in the Marriage Triangle. Then I will show you how to summarize all you have learned about yourself and your relationship by completing the short tests in Chapters Three through Five. This summary of your assessments is called the Marriage Triangle Assessment Summary Sheet. It will help you organize and analyze your results and set goals for improvement in your marital aptitude. By knowing what's in your Marriage Triangle you can take the first step to avoiding its becoming the "Bermuda Triangle of marriage!"

First, take a look at Figure 6.1, which reviews all the factors that predict marital *dissatisfaction*.

Liabilities include problematic *contexts* (for example, young age and parental disapproval), problematic *individual traits* (for example, impulsivity and dysfunctional beliefs), and problematic *couple traits* (for example, short acquaintanceship and poor communication skills). These factors are liabilities you may bring to marriage.

But life isn't made up entirely of liabilities. Figure 6.2 summarizes the assets you may bring to your marriage.

Since these are assets, you will want to have as many of them as you can before you commit yourself to a marriage. The formula for predicting your chances of a

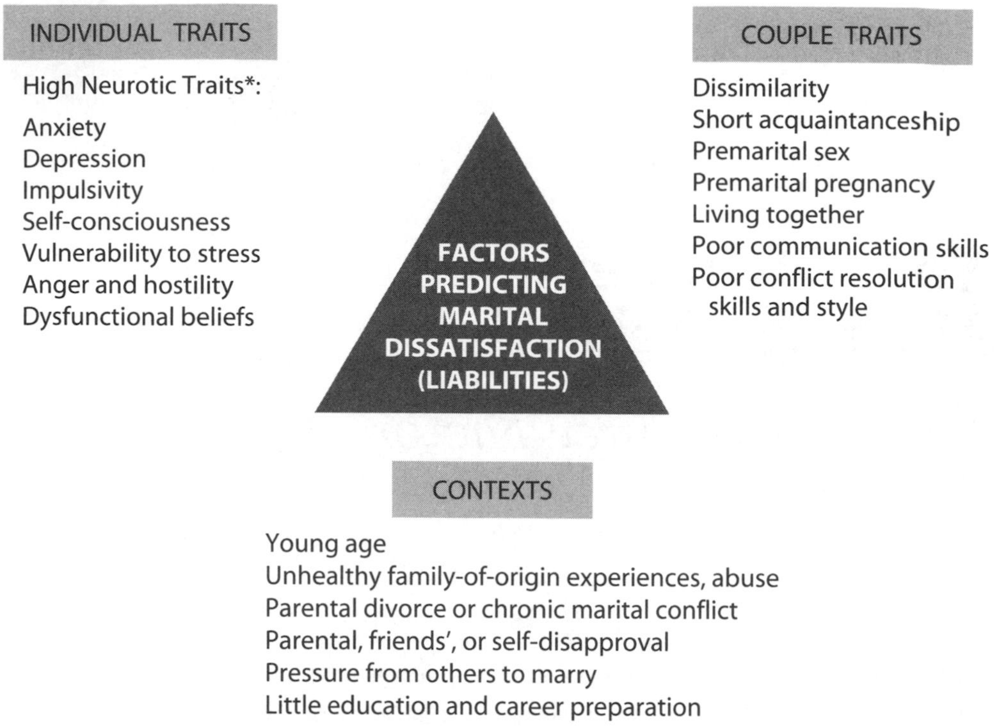

INDIVIDUAL TRAITS

High Neurotic Traits*:

Anxiety
Depression
Impulsivity
Self-consciousness
Vulnerability to stress
Anger and hostility
Dysfunctional beliefs

COUPLE TRAITS

Dissimilarity
Short acquaintanceship
Premarital sex
Premarital pregnancy
Living together
Poor communication skills
Poor conflict resolution
  skills and style

FACTORS
PREDICTING
MARITAL
DISSATISFACTION
(LIABILITIES)

CONTEXTS

Young age
Unhealthy family-of-origin experiences, abuse
Parental divorce or chronic marital conflict
Parental, friends', or self-disapproval
Pressure from others to marry
Little education and career preparation

Figure 6.1. The Downside of the Marriage Triangle

*Individuals with significantly high scores on these traits should seek further assessment and treatment by a licensed therapist.

satisfying marriage consists of the ratio of assets to liabilities that you bring to marriage. The higher your ratio, the better your chances for success. First, let's look at three examples of how to use the summary sheet—then we'll calculate your ratio for each dimension of the Marriage Triangle.

🕏 Using the Summary Sheet

The first example shows the results of the summary Vince (twenty-seven) prepared and his plan for strengthening his Marriage Triangle. (See Figure 6.3.) He was con-

INDIVIDUAL TRAITS

High self-esteem
Flexibility
Assertiveness
Sociability

COUPLE TRAITS

Similarity
Long acquaintanceship
Good communication skills
Good conflict resolutions
  skills and style

FACTORS PREDICTING MARITAL SATISFACTION (ASSETS)

CONTEXTS

Older age
Healthy family-of-origin experiences
Happy parental marriage
Parental and friends' approval
Significant education and career preparation

Figure 6.2. Hopeful Indicators in the Marriage Triangle

sidering an engagement to Barbara (twenty-four) at the time he read this material and completed his short tests.

Notice that Vince rated only one dimension of the triangle with a positive asset to liability ratio: contexts. His age and family background were assets, and his parents highly approved of his marriage plans. However, they were pressuring him a bit too much to get married. They dreaded the thought of having a son who was almost thirty who was still single. In their social circle, young men were usually married by age twenty-five unless there was "something wrong" with them. Vince was struggling to finish his master's degree in English and did not have a firm career direction.

His ratio of assets and liabilities in individual traits was equal, and thus, he rated this overall area as neither an asset nor a liability but rather as undecided.

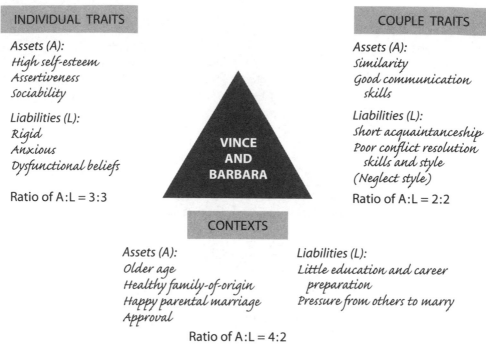

Assets (A):
High self-esteem
Assertiveness
Sociability

Liabilities (L):
Rigid
Anxious
Dysfunctional beliefs

Ratio of A:L = 3:3

COUPLE TRAITS

Assets (A):
Similarity
Good communication
 skills

Liabilities (L):
Short acquaintanceship
Poor conflict resolution
 skills and style
 (Neglect style)

Ratio of A:L = 2:2

VINCE
AND
BARBARA

CONTEXTS

Assets (A):
Older age
Healthy family-of-origin
Happy parental marriage
Approval

Liabilities (L):
Little education and career
 preparation
Pressure from others to marry

Ratio of A:L = 4:2
Overall Ratio = 9:7

Figure 6.3. Example One: Vince's Triangle

Although he had good self-esteem, sociability, and assertiveness, his short test results showed him to be significantly more rigid and anxious than the norm group. And two dysfunctional beliefs were partially responsible for his anxiety and were related to his conflict resolution problems with Barbara: "Disagreements in marriage are destructive" and "People don't change." Whenever Barbara strongly disagreed with him these two beliefs were activated—that is, he would think, "Since disagreements are bad and she won't change anyway, it's best just to avoid a confrontation here." This made him feel anxious because Barbara kept trying to get him to talk. His strategy was to ignore the problem or try to escape from it. This is a good example of how thoughts, feelings, and behavior fit together to explain how a person reacts in a stressful situation. Vince knew that unless he changed these beliefs his anxiety would automatically cut in whenever Barbara raised an issue and he would use the same destructive type of conflict resolution—neglect.

Finally, his ratio of couple assets and liabilities was also equal and so he rated the overall area as undecided. Although similarities and good communication skills helped them get along most of the time, their lack of healthy conflict resolution skills was a serious area of concern for him. Their short acquaintanceship was another source of his anxiety.

So, overall, Vince's Marriage Triangle looked slightly positive—one asset area (contexts) and two mixed areas (individual and couple traits) and an overall ratio of 9:7—nine assets to seven liabilities. He admitted that although things were going well with them, it was not time to get married yet—there were too many liabilities present. Exhibit 6.1 shows how Vince listed the areas he wanted to strengthen before considering marriage and developed an action plan. After four months of counseling with a therapist and the support and efforts of Barbara, too, they were engaged.

Figure 6.4 shows a second example of using the summary sheet. In this case, the couple was Scott (twenty-six) and Mary (twenty). Mary is the one who filled out the assessment.

Mary's evaluation of her contexts showed an absence of assets and several liabilities. She had just turned twenty years old and had just begun her education and career planning. She came from a family where she was emotionally neglected due to her parents' frequent marital conflicts and divorce. This created exaggerated self-consciousness in her—she always questioned her physical appearance and attractiveness to others, especially men. Her mother had too few opportunities to reassure her of her appearance and worth as she was growing up due to her own depression and divorce. When a man did give Mary some special attention she was drawn to it like a moth to a candle. This led her to sometimes impulsively engage in sex with Scott, which was contrary to her values. Her mother discovered this and worried that this "older man" was just using her daughter sexually and taking advantage of her impulsive nature and self-consciousness. Hence, she strongly disapproved of the relationship.

Mary admitted that so far the relationship was mostly driven by sex, and that she and Scott were really very dissimilar in age, religion, and many of their values. When they discussed their dissimilarities, they did so effectively and conflicts were

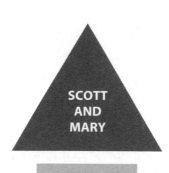

INDIVIDUAL TRAITS

Assets (A):
Flexibility
Assertiveness
Sociability

Liabilities (L):
Self-consciousness
Impulsiveness

Ratio of A : L = 3 : 2

COUPLE TRAITS

Assets (A):
Good communication skills
Good conflict resolutions
 skills and style

Liabilities (L):
Dissimilarity
Short acquaintanceship
Premarital sex

Ratio of A : L = 2 : 3

SCOTT
AND
MARY

CONTEXTS

Assets (A):   *Liabilities (L)*
None   *Young age*
                   Unhealthy family-of-origin
                   Parental marital conflict and divorce
                   Disapproval
                   Little education and career preparation

Ratio of A : L = 0 : 5
Overall Ratio = 5 : 10

Figure 6.4. Example Two: Mary's Triangle

generally resolved through discussion and compromise, but due to their many differences, these discussions occurred with such regularity that Mary asked me, "Is it normal to have so many strong disagreements when you've only known a guy two months?" I said, "No!"

Thus Mary rated her triangle as consisting of one asset area and two liability areas. Her ratio of assets to liabilities was a miserable 5:10—not very good odds, overall, for pursuing marriage! Exhibit 6.2 shows how she listed the areas to strengthen before marriage, and the plan she developed.

After a month of hard work on this plan, Mary decided the task was simply too great—there were just too many problems to resolve. Soon thereafter, she and Scott broke up and are both happily dating other people today.

The third example of using the summary sheet is a bit different. I decided to look back and assess my own Marriage Triangle based on what I remember about myself (then age twenty-three), my wife Jeannie (twenty-two), and our relationship before our marriage. Figure 6.5 shows my summary sheet.

My results for contexts show several assets and no liabilities. I rated my family-of-origin experiences as healthy and my parents' marriage as happy. My family was a safe, secure, and nurturing place in which to grow up. My parents never pressured me to marry but approved of the idea when I mentioned it. I had finished my four-year college degree and had my career direction firmly decided even before meeting Jeannie. Looking back, it seems that we were a bit young to marry, but not so young that it was a liability for us.

As an individual I rated myself as fairly normal. (Surprise!?) Two personality traits have been great assets to me in our marriage: flexibility and sociability. These traits make me easier to get along with and help me compromise. A personal liability was my dysfunctional belief that my wife should magically know what I wanted without my saying it (the ESP myth). This left Jeannie to guess what was on my mind—which led to frustration on my part that she was not guessing right! It also limited my self-disclosure, which made me seem distant to her at times.

As a couple we were very similar on life's most important values, age, family backgrounds, and religion. By the time we married we had known each other for about fourteen months. (Yes, I did take her and some other friends camping and we did have the usual camping crises including getting lost in the dark on the way to the camp site!) I rated our communication skills as a liability, but this was mostly my problem, not hers. I needed to work on self-disclosing more deeply and more often, and on being a better listener. So, overall, I rated my Marriage Triangle as having three assets and no liabilities (my overall ratio was 9:2). If I had to do it all over again, I would have set up a plan like the one in Exhibit 6.3.

Looking back and doing this assessment after twenty-seven years of satisfying marriage was interesting and validating. Jeannie and I had the "right stuff" to get married and stay happily married. That does not mean our marriage has been perfect (no honest person has a perfect marriage!), or without strains here and there. Nor does my example mean that your ratio of assets to liabilities must be at least 9:2 for you to have a satisfying marriage. But, as I said earlier, be sure the odds (ratio) are in your favor when you gamble on marriage.

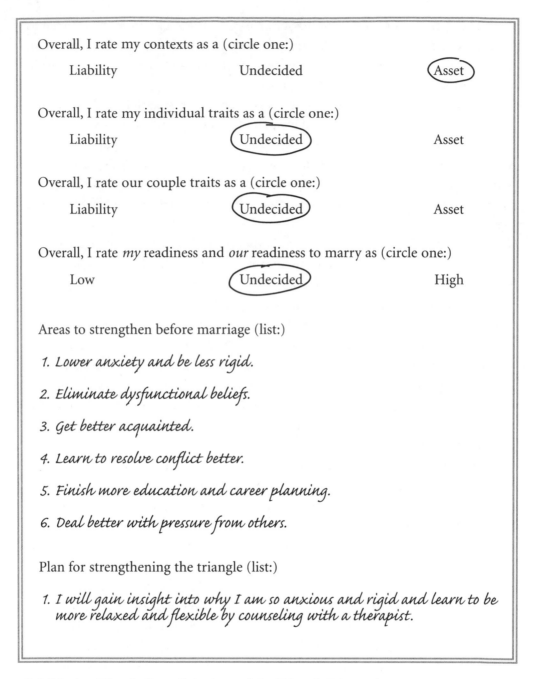

Overall, I rate my contexts as a (circle one:)

    Liability   Undecided   (Asset)

Overall, I rate my individual traits as a (circle one:)

    Liability   (Undecided)   Asset

Overall, I rate our couple traits as a (circle one:)

    Liability   (Undecided)   Asset

Overall, I rate *my* readiness and *our* readiness to marry as (circle one:)

    Low   (Undecided)   High

Areas to strengthen before marriage (list:)

1. Lower anxiety and be less rigid.

2. Eliminate dysfunctional beliefs.

3. Get better acquainted.

4. Learn to resolve conflict better.

5. Finish more education and career planning.

6. Deal better with pressure from others.

Plan for strengthening the triangle (list:)

1. I will gain insight into why I am so anxious and rigid and learn to be more relaxed and flexible by counseling with a therapist.

Exhibit 6.1. Vince's Overall Ratings of the Triangle Dimensions

2. I will challenge dysfunctional beliefs and develop more functional beliefs by counseling with a therapist.

3. I will discuss with Barbara the importance of a longer acquaintance-ship and set a goal with her to get better acquainted before consider-ing marriage.

4. Barbara and I will discuss how we can learn better conflict resolution skills and improve on the neglect style we currently use, which is not working. We need to stop ignoring and refusing to discuss our prob-lems. This may involve assistance from our clergyman or attending a conflict resolution skills training program.

5. Barbara and I will plan our future marriage, should it occur, so that we both have completed as much education and career preparation as possible.

6. I will discuss with my therapist how to better deal with the pressure my parents are putting on us to get married.

Exhibit 6.1. *Continued*

Overall, I rate my contexts as a (circle one:)

    (Liability)   Undecided   Asset

Overall, I rate my individual traits as a (circle one:)

    Liability   Undecided   (Asset)

Overall, I rate our couple traits as a (circle one:)

    (Liability)   Undecided   Asset

Overall, I rate *my* readiness and *our* readiness to marry as (circle one:)

    Low   Undecided   (High)

Areas to strengthen before marriage (list:)

1. Deal with negative emotions and attitudes related to parents' marital problems and neglect of me.

2. I need to be older, more mature, and closer to completing my education and career plans.

3. Seek parental approval.

4. Reexamine our dissimilarities and their long-term effects on us as a couple if we were to marry.

5. Become better acquainted.

6. Examine the role of premarital sex in our relationship.

7. Overcome my self-consciousness and impulsivity.

Exhibit 6.2. Mary's Overall Ratings of the Triangle Dimensions

Plan for strengthening the triangle (list:)

1. *Overcome negative effects of parents' marital conflict, divorce, and neglect by counseling with a therapist.*

2. *Strengthen my self-confidence and control my impulsivity by counseling with a therapist.*

3. *Confront our dissimilarities more honestly and resolve them.*

4. *Get better acquainted in relationship areas other than sex.*

5. *Get more education and career preparation completed.*

6. *Seek mother's approval of our relationship through calm discussions with her.*

Exhibit 6.2. *Continued*

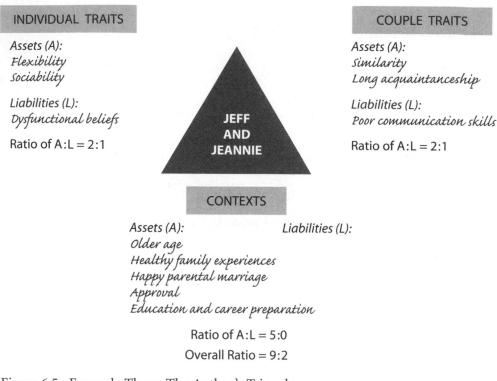

INDIVIDUAL TRAITS

Assets (A):
Flexibility
Sociability

Liabilities (L):
Dysfunctional beliefs

Ratio of A:L = 2:1

COUPLE TRAITS

Assets (A):
Similarity
Long acquaintanceship

Liabilities (L):
Poor communication skills

Ratio of A:L = 2:1

JEFF
AND
JEANNIE

CONTEXTS

Assets (A):   Liabilities (L):
Older age
Healthy family experiences
Happy parental marriage
Approval
Education and career preparation

Ratio of A:L = 5:0
Overall Ratio = 9:2

Figure 6.5. Example Three: The Author's Triangle

Completing Your Own Summary Sheet

Now, it's time for you to develop your own summary sheet. Follow these steps:

1. In the spaces provided in Figure 6.6, list your assets and liabilities from Chapters Three through Five.

2. Figure your ratios of assets to liabilities for each dimension of the triangle. Write them in the spaces provided.

3. Make your overall ratings of the three dimensions.

4. Rate your overall readiness to marry in Exhibit 6.4.

Overall, I rate my contexts as a (circle one:)

    Liability   Undecided   (Asset)

Overall, I rate my individual traits as a (circle one:)

    Liability   Undecided   (Asset)

Overall, I rate our couple traits as a (circle one:)

    Liability   Undecided   (Asset)

Overall, I rate *my* readiness and *our* readiness to marry as (circle one:)

    (Low)   Undecided   High

Areas to strengthen before marriage (list:)

1. Eliminate dysfunctional ESP belief.

2. Learn communication skills.

Plan for strengthening the triangle (list:)

1. Challenge my dysfunctional ESP belief and develop a more functional belief by counseling with a trusted older friend who is a psychologist.

2. Read self-help books about the importance of self-disclosure in marriage.

3. Participate in a couple communication skills training course at the university.

Exhibit 6.3. The Author's Overall Ratings of the Triangle Dimensions

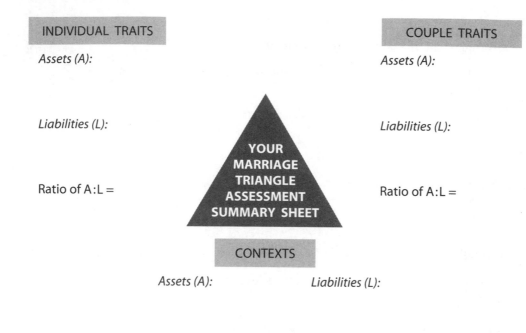

INDIVIDUAL TRAITS

Assets (A):

Liabilities (L):

Ratio of A:L =

COUPLE TRAITS

Assets (A):

Liabilities (L):

Ratio of A:L =

YOUR
MARRIAGE
TRIANGLE
ASSESSMENT
SUMMARY SHEET

CONTEXTS

Assets (A):   Liabilities (L):

Ratio of A:L =
Overall Ratio =

Figure 6.6. The Reader's Triangle

5. List the areas to strengthen before marriage. Be specific.

6. Develop your plans for how you will strengthen these areas. (Specific resources you can draw on are found in Chapter Eight.)

What are the best solutions for strengthening areas that need improvement? For example, self-help books are useful in some areas (see Chapter Eight). Counseling with a trusted friend or clergy person works better for harder problems (for example, individual problems and couple problems). Professional therapy is usually necessary for more chronic and serious individual and couple problems (for example, depression and destructive conflict resolution styles). Finally, skills development programs are very useful when trying to improve such techniques as

Overall, I rate my contexts as a (circle one:)

    Liability   Undecided   Asset

Overall, I rate my individual traits as a (circle one:)

    Liability   Undecided   Asset

Overall, I rate our couple traits as a (circle one:)

    Liability   Undecided   Asset

Overall, I rate *my* readiness and *our* readiness to marry as (circle one:)

    Low   Undecided   High

Areas to strengthen before marriage (list:)

Plan for strengthening the triangle (list:)

Exhibit 6.4. The Reader's Overall Ratings of the Triangle Dimensions

empathic listening, clear sending, and conflict resolution. More details on these types of skills development programs are described in Chapter Eight.

Share your results and plans with your partner as appropriate. Ask for your partner's opinion and advice. What plans will involve active participation with you (for example, improving conflict resolution skills)?

Before going to Chapter Eight for specific resources, let's first look more closely at types of people and circumstances that should be taken as red lights in your relationship. So far in this book, I've given you several yellow caution lights *(go slow)* and a couple of red lights *(stop!)* when discussing risky situations in which you may find yourself (for example, parental lack of approval). In Chapter Seven I will give you examples of select partners and relationship circumstances that require red lights *(stop!)*. Red lights appear when it is important for you to stop what you're currently doing or stop (that is, strongly consider ending) the relationship. I hope these red lights will be enlightening and useful to you as you navigate through relationships in your life.

#

SEVEN

Whom and When Not to Marry!

He seemed really caring at first—always wanted to know what I was doing. It was really kind of flattering! But then he started telling me what to do and after a while I felt trapped!

—Teresa, twenty-nine-year-old nurse

The first time it happened we were coming out of a dance club. A guy just looked over at me for a few seconds and Jared came unglued! He hit the guy and it took all four of us to pull him off!

—Janie, twenty-three-year-old college student

He would stand in the doorway and not let me leave the room until I apologized.

—Cherise, twenty-five-year-old waitress

When we got serious she started complaining about the time I spent with my buddies. She criticized my friends more. It was like none of them were good enough now.

—Gene, twenty-three-year-old law student

Some individuals possess personality or behavioral characteristics that are especially troublesome in a relationship and suggest more serious underlying problems that make those people difficult if not dangerous to live with. Many of them have exaggerated neurotic traits like anger or anxiety. These people usually have little insight into their problems and seldom change much even in therapy. That's why they are so important for you to recognize as poor marriage choices. The opening quotes give quick glimpses of four types of these individuals. Let's diagnose each person or situation highlighted there and see why they should be identified as red lights *(stop!)* if you encounter them.

ℰ Types to Avoid

Teresa's boyfriend showed traits of a controller. He easily became anxious and jealous of her spending time with others. He even resented her spending time alone! *Don't get married to a controller!*

Janie's boyfriend was very jealous and an anger addict—he would explode like a bomb whenever it appeared to him that other men were flirting with her. (Others in her group frequently said, "That guy wasn't flirting with you!") *Don't get married to an anger addict!*

Cherise was in an abusive relationship with her boyfriend. Do you know the signs of abuse? They include acts such as these:

- Hitting, kicking, slapping, pushing, pinching, hair pulling, grabbing too hard, throwing objects, and restraining someone against their will—*physical abuse.*
- Name-calling, ridicule, insults, inappropriate teasing, threatening with a gun or knife or other object, threatening to leave forever, threatening to kill oneself or someone else, and stalking—*emotional abuse.*
- Forcing you to do things you don't want to, especially sexually—*domination and sexual abuse.*

And no! Your partner will not stop doing it after you're married. You'll only see more of the same. *Don't get married to an abuser!*

Gene had an overly possessive girlfriend. Due to her anxiety and low self-esteem, she had to have him all to herself. That may sound flattering at first, but eventually it's not. You feel forced to give up all your old friends and interests to live with a person obsessed with you. *Don't get married to a possessor!*

✥ Red Light Indicators

Here's a list of other individuals and relationship situations that should be red lights to you. *Don't get married in any of these situations:*[1]

- If either of you is frequently (relentlessly) asking, "Are you *sure* you love me? Do you *really* care about me?" People who fall into this pattern are *approval types.* These individuals have such poor self-esteem that you can never tell them often enough how much you care about them for them to believe it. They need therapy, not marriage, in which case you'll both need professional help!

- If, when you are together, you spend most of your time disagreeing and quarreling with no resolution. You're in a *love-hate relationship.* The quarreling will only get worse after marriage when additional stress is added to your lives.

- If you don't get along well with either your mother or father, and your prospective mate seems to you to be just like that troublesome parent. If you did not like those traits in a parent, you will like them even less in a spouse!

- If you are really marrying someone to mother or father you. When you think more carefully about it, does your partner really seem more like a big brother or big sister to you? Are you getting a lot of parenting from your partner? Does your partner feed your self-esteem and make up for what Mom or Dad failed to do? Satisfying marriages occur between equals, not a parent and a child.

- If you keep thinking, "Maybe things will get better after we're married." They usually don't!

- If your mate-to-be claims to approve of your interests and activities but then criticizes you for spending so much time on them. Behavior speaks louder than words! If you are unsure of your partner's real feelings and intentions, watch behavior, not words. If they do not match, point out the inconsistency. But don't marry someone who's doing this to you!

- If, after you've done some soul-searching, you discover that you are marrying a sex object rather than a person. Is your relationship primarily a sexual one? If so, that is no reason to marry. Decide if you want to get to know the rest of the person first.

- If you spend a day alone with your prospective mate (without watching television), and you find it intolerable. Sounds funny, right? But take away all the entertainment the two of you enjoy together, the socializing with friends and so on, and ask yourself how well you really know this person. One-on-one, perhaps things are not all that great.

- If you are rebounding from your last love relationship. Deal with your pain from a previous relationship with the help of a friend, clergy person, or therapist instead. Wait at least one year between serious relationships so you can heal. Don't do amateur psychotherapy instead with someone else in a new relationship. Don't get into a new relationship until you are healed from the last one.

- If your partner is an addict and not in recovery. Addictions may occur with alcohol, drugs, sex, eating, gambling, spending, work, exercise, and many other factors. See Washton and Boundy's *Willpower's Not Enough* for an explanation of how a normal person can become addicted to a substance or activity and how to get into a recovery program.[2] And if your addict is in recovery, don't marry until he or she has demonstrated at least one year of sobriety and is committed to maintaining sobriety for life. Here again, behavior speaks louder than words.

- If your partner is just the opposite of you. Be intrigued, but don't marry! Intriguing traits (say, "thrifty") become nuisances ("tightwad") after marriage. Focus on similarities, not differences.

- If he appears to be the "strong, silent type." These men are usually silent for unhealthy reasons like an abusive past, an alcoholic parent, poor self-esteem, or a lack of emotional awareness. The silence will drive you crazy!

- If she is a perfectionist. She will drive both of you crazy!

- If your partner has traits you cannot stand (such as poor grooming habits) but you never raise the issue for fear of offending. Yes, little things can drive you crazy, too! They will drive you crazier if you get married.

- If you frequently feel manipulated. Manipulators are dishonest, selfish, and play dirty. If they can't get what they want up front (by asking), they resort to guerilla tactics to trick you or coerce you into doing things their way (threatening you, whining, guilt-tripping, and so on through an endless list).

- If your partner overreacts to simple problems or situations. Others will notice this, too, and comment to you with phrases like, "What's going on?" Someone who seems wound too tight may be emotionally unstable (for example, highly neurotic).

- If you find yourself being too anxious to please a partner who gives little back in return. Exaggerated selfishness in your partner is very difficult to change. We call such people *narcissistic.* They will get their needs met first, and then, if they have time left over, they *may* consider your feelings and needs. But don't count on it. You end up feeling neglected.

- If you're desperately lonely. Get a dog or cat instead. And pursue professional therapy as soon as possible!

- If you and your partner have a chronic pattern of breaking up and getting back together. Such premarital relationship instability should be evidence to you that your relationship will never survive the greater rigors of marriage. Keep dating if you like, but do not get married!

- If either of you have a history of loving your partner one day and hating them the next, unexplained big mood swings, or manipulative behaviors (for example, unfairly threatening to leave your partner if you don't get what you want). Such traits suggest that you need therapy, not an intimate relationship. People with these traits simply "cannot do relationships."

- If marriage looks like a way to improve yourself. Sloppy people sometimes marry neat people to help themselves become neater. Alcoholics often marry professional or amateur nurses. Shy individuals marry party animals. Two years later, they are all divorced! Improve yourself before marriage using self-help materials, trusted friends, clergy, therapists, and of course, good, hard work. Marry when you're whole.

- If you're in an unequal relationship. Inequality is exhibited by such traits as these:

  Her opinion is more important than your opinion when you're discussing important couple decisions.
  He seldom compromises with you when the two of you disagree.
  She wins most of the debates or arguments.
  He makes most of the major decisions—especially those that should involve

you equally—choosing where to live, birth control, how to manage money, and so on.

Her needs are given preference to your needs, nearly always.

He says he wants a marriage of equals, but his behavior does not reflect this attitude.

You find yourself frequently giving in "to keep the peace."

- If your self-esteem suffers as a result of being in the relationship, or you feel neglected— "but it's better than nothing." You will feel worse after marriage and learn too late that nothing probably *was* better than this.

- If your partner brings out the worst qualities or behavior in you, not the best in you. When you're together, do you try to exhibit your best qualities—good manners, respect, treating your partner as an equal? Or do you find yourself being critical, not listening well, being sloppy with your grooming or dress, or exhibiting other unfortunate aspects of your personality?

- If you frequently feel misunderstood and are constantly trying to explain your point of view or how you feel. Your partner may lack more than listening skills, and may have no interest in understanding you. Marriage will not magically solve this problem.

- If your partner was previously married—unless at least one year has passed since the divorce and the emotional healing process is largely complete.

This last point is very important. People react to divorce similarly to a death—with much emotional turmoil, even if they instigated the divorce. It takes most people at least a year to grieve the loss of a relationship, resolve who was at fault, get over feelings of failure and guilt, adjust to new relationships with their children (especially for a noncustodial parent) and help them grieve appropriately, and resolve the financial difficulties that usually occur in a divorce. Remember, divorce is rated just behind the death of a loved one as one of life's greatest stressors. Give your divorced partner the time to grieve, heal, and get to know you, slowly, without rebounding. Don't let anyone talk you into an intense rebound relationship—one driven principally by an escape from loneliness and the need for affection and validation.

The key characteristics of the people or situations described in this chapter—the ones that should make your approach to them a red light—is this: *they do not change easily or quickly.* So unless you have a lot of time and patience and a high level of commitment from your partner to change—with behavioral evidence to back it up—just avoid these kinds of people and situations. There are too many healthier people and situations out there to settle for one of these. And, remember, your chances for marital failure with these kinds of individuals or situations is much higher than average. You'll be taking a bigger chance!

Now, let's go to other good resources to help you prepare for marriage. Chapter Eight is a collection of advice and resources to help you improve the condition of your Marriage Triangle and raise your marital aptitude so you will feel more confident about getting married.

EIGHT

Other Resources for Marriage Preparation

Now that you have read this book I hope you are more interested in learning about other resources that will help you prepare yourself and your relationship for a satisfying marriage. The resources described in this chapter include books, courses, programs, and organizations. They are organized, like the rest of this book, by the three dimensions of the Marriage Triangle.

Context Resources

Let's start with the first dimension, your personal and relationship contexts. The resources described here can help you overcome family-of-origin experiences that continue to affect you in negative ways today, and can assist you in dealing with problems with your parents and friends in a healthier and more direct way.

Making Peace with Your Parents by Harold Bloomfield (New York: Random House, 1983). This book contains advice and exercises to help you resolve problematic issues in your life that involve your relationship with your parents, learn to improve communication with your parents, cope with difficult parents, and overcome negative family-of-origin experiences such as divorce, neglect, and abuse. Its message is that *you*, not your family, need to be responsible for overcoming these problems because in the end, the only one you can really change is yourself.

How to Deal with Your Parents by Lynn Osterkamp (New York: Berkley Books, 1992). This book will help you communicate more effectively with your family and get along with them more smoothly. The author helps you set goals for improving relationships and then helps you develop a plan to meet your goals. She also deals with issues such as coping with controlling parents, dealing with disapproval, becoming more autonomous, and avoiding being manipulated.

Right to Innocence: Healing the Trauma of Childhood Sexual Abuse by Beverly Engle (New York: Ivy Books, 1990). This is a classic on how women can overcome the trauma of childhood sexual abuse and change their identity from "victim" to "survivor." It includes step-by-step directions on how to forgive, heal, and go on with your life. It also contains guidelines for parents and friends who can support you.

Victims No Longer: Men Recovering from Incest and Other Childhood Sexual Abuse by Michael Lew (New York: Harper Perennial, 1990). Like *Right to Innocence*, this book helps readers, this time men, overcome the negative effects of sexual abuse on themselves and on their adult relationships.

It Will Never Happen to Me by Claudia Black (New York: Ballantine Books, 1981). Another classic—this time the focus is on assessing the effects of growing up with an alcoholic parent. Black stresses recovering from negative emotional effects and leads the reader through a recovery process in the book.

Willpower's Not Enough: Recovering from Addictions of Every Kind by Arnold Washton and Donna Boundy (New York: Harper Perennial, 1989). Of all the books I have read, this is the best when it comes to explaining to the lay reader how addictions of all kinds may develop and are treated. Great book for those wanting to understand their addict or themselves. It includes a powerful step-by-step procedure for recovering from addictions of all kinds—alcohol, drugs, sex, gambling, spending, eating, exercise, or whatever.

❧ Individual Traits Resources

This section contains recommended resources for building self-esteem, overcoming neurotic traits—especially anxiety, depression, and anger—and changing dysfunctional beliefs about relationships and marriage.

Feeling Good: The New Mood Therapy by David Burns (New York: Avon Books, 1999). This best-seller deserves the acclaim it has received! It explains how depression, anxiety, anger, and low self-esteem develop and are effectively treated using Burns's scientifically tested method of cognitive therapy and coping skills. I have recommended this book to more clients than any other! One of my favorite chapters is titled "Dare to Be Average! Ways to Overcome Perfectionism." Burns shows you step by step how to overcome these emotional problems. His chapter on psychotropic drugs used to treat depression and anxiety is also very informative. The power of this book is that is can be effectively used to treat all six neurotic traits that predict marital dissatisfaction!

Your Perfect Right: A Guide to Assertive Living by Robert Alberti and Michael Emmons (San Luis Obispo, Calif.: Impact, 1990). Another well-deserved best-seller! Learn why you lack assertiveness and how to become more assertive (not aggressive) with others. This includes honest self-expression and directness without hurting others or feeling guilty about it.

Anger: The Misunderstood Emotion by Carol Tavris (New York: Touchstone Books, 1989). This book deals with popular myths about anger, such as "Expressing your anger reduces anger and makes you feel better." Then, Tavris shows you how to develop more functional ways of controlling your anger and dealing with it when it occurs.

A New Guide to Rational Living by Albert Ellis and Robert Harper (Upper Saddle River, N.J.: Prentice Hall, 1975). A classic, like Burns's book, in overcoming dysfunctional beliefs (Ellis calls them "irrational beliefs") and developing more functional or rational beliefs by restructuring your thinking in ways that will lead to more personal and relationship satisfaction.

Why Love Is Not Enough by Sol Gordon (Boston: Bob Adams, 1988). This book will help you dispel myths about marriage and show you a more realistic look at what makes marriage work—it does take more than love. (You know that now, right?) Gordon explains immature versus mature love, asks you to determine your motives for marriage, lists questions you should ask your partner before getting serious, and so on. It's a very provocative and useful book!

🕸 Couple Traits Resources

I emphasized earlier that communication and conflict resolution skills are among the best predictors of later marital satisfaction. You can improve your skills by reading and practicing the principles in the books I list here, or by participating in a communication skills training program at your local college, church, synagogue, YMCA, or YWCA. Most important, I list programs specifically designed for premarital couples and with scientific support for their validity. In addition, I list some of the best overall premarital preparation books and programs I have studied. Let's start with communication skills training books and programs that will strengthen your relationship now and better prepare you for marriage.

The Prevention and Relationship Enhancement Program (PREP) is based on twenty years of research, which has shown that couples who successfully participate in this six-week program have lower rates of break-up and divorce and report more satisfying relationships, less negative communication patterns, and higher levels of positive communication as a result of the program. PREP is traditionally offered in weekend workshops or in six weekly sessions of two hours each. For more information about the program, contact:

PREP, Inc.
Box 102530
Denver, CO 80250-2530
(303) 759-9931
E-mail: prepinc@aol.com
Web site: www.PREPinc.com

The PREP office can also send you a list of audio and video tapes that focus on helping couples preserve and enhance their marriages by teaching communication and conflict resolution skills, deepening love, friendship, fun, sensuality, and commitment.

Fighting for Your Marriage: Positive Steps for Preventing Divorce and Preserving a Lasting Love by Howard Markman, Scott Stanley, and Susan L. Blumberg (San Francisco: Jossey-Bass, 1994) contains the entire content of the PREP program. Order it to get a start on the program on your own.

A second communication program based on solid research is called *Great Start*. This impressive program combines the *Couple Communication* program and the *PREPARE/ENRICH* relationship inventories to help you launch your marriage successfully and keep it vital. Couples first complete the PREPARE instrument (similar to the RELATE) and complete the Couple Communication I program, in which they learn speaking, listening, conflict resolution, and styles of communication skills. These activities are done in a workshop format with a trained group leader. After a year of marriage, couples complete the ENRICH inventory and Couple Communication II, where they learn how to manage relationship stages and anger, correct dissatisfying communication patterns, and so on. So Great Start gives you and your partner a one-two (premarital and postmarital) combination of relationship assessment and skills training. I highly recommend this program. For information on Great Start write to:

Great Start
7201 S. Broadway
Suite #210
Littleton, CO 80122
(800) 328-5099
E-mail: icp@comskills.com
Web site: www.couplecommunication.com

Connecting with Self and Others by Sherod Miller, Daniel Wackman, Elam Nunnally, and Phyllis Miller (Littleton, Colo.: Interpersonal Communication Programs, 1989) is an excellent book written by the authors of the Couple Communication program. In addition to teaching communication and conflict resolution skills, it includes interesting chapters on how to communicate effectively in stressful situations with others who want to fight or act spitefully, and about relationship stages and personality dynamics in relationships.

Another research-based communication skills training program is called *Relationship Enhancement (RE)*. Couples learn speaking, listening, conflict resolution, self-change, helping others change, and other skills during this workshop. The RE program most recently developed a home study version wherein couples get four hours of private coaching from a trained coach on the telephone. It is referred to as PhoneCoach. RE is a very effective program and I recommend it to you. For more information contact:

National Institute of Relationship Enhancement
(800) 4-FAMILIES

E-mail: niremd@nire.org
Web site: www.nire.org

Another relationship skills course, which has recently been scientifically validated, is called *PAIRS FIRST* (Practical Application of Intimate Relationship Skills). It is an eight-session course focused on communication skills, conflict resolution skills, understanding self and others, and the logic of love and emotions. For more information about this program contact:

PAIRS International, Inc.
PMB 158, 318 Indian Trace
Weston, FL 33326
(888) PAIRS-4U (724-7748)
E-mail: info@pairs.com
Web site: www.pairs.com

I recommend these two books on preparing for marriage:

Saving Your Marriage Before It Starts by Les Parrott and Leslie Parrott (Grand Rapids, Mich.: Zondervan, 1995). This book addresses seven key relationship areas by posing "Seven Questions to Ask Before (or After) You Marry." These are some of the questions: Have you faced the myths of marriage with honesty? Can you identify your love style? Have you bridged the gender gap? Can you say what you mean and understand what you hear?

Finding the Love of Your Life by Neil Warren (Colorado Springs, Colo.: Focus on the Family, 1992). Warren's premise is that there is skill involved in mate selection. This book is filled with excellent advice including eliminating the seven most prevalent causes of faulty mate selection, getting yourself healthy before marriage, and letting passionate love mature before you marry.

Finally, here is a book about self-help books:

The Authoritative Guide to Self-Help Books by John Sautrock, Ann Minnett, and Barbara Campbell (New York: Guilford Press, 1994). This book lists the best (according to a national survey of five hundred psychologists) self-help books available up to the time it was published, on thirty-two different subjects including abuse and recovery, anger, depression, anxiety, assertiveness, communication, the family, love, intimacy, and marriage. It's a good resource for finding books to help yourself or a loved one. Many of the books I recommend here are reviewed in this manual.

To get more information on preparing for marriage and enriching existing marriages you should contact a new organization: the *Coalition for Marriage, Family, and Couples Education (CMFCE)*. This organization's goal is "to increase the availability of skill-based marriage education courses in the community." CMFCE defines its audience as single young adults like you, saying: "they've watched their parents, neighbors, grandparents, teachers, coaches, and ministers divorce—and they are eager for new information that will help them do things differently" (Directory of Youth and School-Based Marriage Education Programs, 1999).[1] The CMFCE network disseminates detailed information about many premarital education programs, books, videos, audiotapes, premarital counseling resources, and workshops around the country. It is a marriage preparation gold mine! You may contact the network in several ways:

CMFCE
5310 Belt Road, NW
Washington, DC 20015-1961
(202) 362-3332
Web site: www.smartmarriages.com
E-mail: CMFCE@smartmarriages.com

If you need a referral for premarital counseling or individual therapy, contact:

American Association for Marriage and Family Therapy (AAMFT)
1133 15th Street, NW
Suite 300
Washington, DC 20005-2710
(202) 452-0109
Web site: www.aamft.org

The AAMFT has a national directory of qualified premarital and marital therapists. Regardless of the type of therapist you see (psychologist, marriage and family therapist, professional counselor, social worker, or pastoral counselor), be sure he or she is licensed in your state and has specialized training in premarital assessment, premarital counseling, and marital therapy approaches. Not all therapists have this specialized training.

In Conclusion

So you have come far in your journey to learn what factors predict a satisfying marriage, assessing yourself and your relationship based on these factors, and planning how to improve your marital aptitude and readiness for marriage. It is my sincerest hope that as a result, you will be the right person, marry the right person, and marry at the right time in your life. Marriage is too precious and important to us all to not educate and prepare ourselves for it the best we possibly can.

As a result of reading this book and others I have suggested, I hope you will join me in the cause of educating the young adults of America about marriage and helping them to be more prepared for this most challenging but most fulfilling of life's relationships. My best wishes to you for a satisfying and stable marriage!

Let me end this book with one of my favorite cartoons about premarital education. It speaks for itself!

Note: Used with permission of Pat Bagly, June 18, 1999.

Notes

Introduction

1. Holman, T. B., Busby, D. M., Doxey, C., Klein, D. M., & Loyer-Carlson, V. (1997). *The RELATionship Evaluation.* Provo, UT: Center for Family Studies.

Chapter 1

1. Ellis, A. (1976). Techniques of handling anger in marriage. *Journal of Marriage and Family Counseling, 2,* 305–316.
2. Gordon, S. (1988). *Why love is not enough.* Boston: Bob Adams.
3. Walster E., & Walster, G. W. (1978). *A new look at love.* Reading, MA: Addison-Wesley.
4. Lazarus, A. A. (1985). *Marital myths.* San Luis Obispo, CA: Impact.
5. Lederer, W., & Jackson, D. (1968). *The mirages of marriage.* New York: Norton.
6. Mace, D. R. (1983). *Prevention in family services: Approaches to family wellness.* Thousand Oaks, CA: Sage.

Chapter 2

1. Doxey, C., & Larson, J. H. (1977). *The RELATE Report.* Provo, UT: Family Studies Center.

Chapter 3

1. Gottman, J. (1994). *Why marriages succeed or fail.* New York: Simon & Schuster.
2. Gottman, *Why marriages succeed or fail.* Quote in this paragraph is from p. 45.

3. Gottman, *Why marriages succeed or fail.* Quote in this paragraph is from p. 37.

4. Amato, P. R. (1996). Explaining the intergenerational transmission of divorce. *Journal of Marriage and the Family, 58,* 628–640.

5. Amato, Explaining the intergenerational transmission of divorce.

6. Amato, Explaining the intergenerational transmission of divorce.

7. Amato, Explaining the intergenerational transmission of divorce.

8. Martin, T. C., & Bumpass, L. L. (1989). Recent trends in marital disruption. *Demography, 26,* 37–51.

9. Heaton, T. B. (1998). Factors contributing to increasing marital stability in the United States. Paper submitted for publication.

10. Kurdek, L. A. (1993). Predicting marital dissolution: A five-year prospective longitudinal study of newlywed couples. *Journal of Personality and Social Psychology, 64,* 221–242.

11. Warren, N. (1992). *Finding the love of your life.* Colorado Springs, CO: Focus on the Family.

12. Warren, *Finding the love of your life.*

13. Warren, *Finding the love of your life,* pp. 150–151.

14. Cline, V. B. (1987). *How to make a good marriage great.* New York: Walker, p. 6.

Chapter 4

1. Kurdek, L. A. (1993). Predicting marital dissolution: A five-year prospective longitudinal study of newlywed couples. *Journal of Personality and Social Psychology, 64,* 221–242.

2. Baucom, D., & Epstein, N. (1990). *Cognitive behavioral marital therapy.* New York: Taylor & Francis, pp. 442–444.

3. McCrae, R. R., & Costa, P. T. (1990). *Personality in adulthood.* New York: Guilford Press.

4. Warren, N. (1992). *Finding the love of your life.* Colorado Springs, CO: Focus on the Family.

5. Baucom, D., & Epstein, N. (1990). *Cognitive behavioral marital therapy.* New York: Taylor & Francis.

6. Wright, L. M., Watson, W. L., & Bell, J. M. (1996). *Beliefs: The heart of healing families and illness.* New York: Basic Books, p. 5.

7. Maxmen, J. S., & Ward, N. G. (1995). *Essential psychopathology and its treatment* (2nd ed.). New York: Norton.

8. Warren, *Finding the love of your life,* p. 78.

9. Canary, D. J., & Emmers-Sommer, T. M. (1997). *Sex and gender differences in personal relationships.* New York: Guilford Press.

10. Gottman, J. (1994). *Why marriages succeed or fail.* New York: Simon & Schuster.

Chapter 5

1. Rusbult, C. E., Johnson, D. J., & Morrow, G. D. (1986). Impact of couple patterns of problem solving on distress and nondistress in dating relationships. *Journal of Personality and Social Psychology, 50,* 744–753.

2. Warren, N. (1992). *Finding the love of your life.* Colorado Springs, CO: Focus on the Family.

3. Based on Joanning, H., Brewster, J., & Koval, J. (1984). The communication rapid assessment scale: Development of a behavioral index of communication quality. *Journal of Marital and Family Therapy, 10,* 409–417.

4. Gottman, J., and Silver, N. (1999). *The seven principles for making marriage work.* New York: Crown.

5. Whyte, M. K. (1990). *Dating, mating, and marriage.* New York: Aldine.

6. Warren, *Finding the love of your life,* p. 9.

7. Laumann, E. O., Gagnon, J. H., Michael, R. T., & Michaels, S. (1994). *The social organization of sexuality.* Chicago: University of Chicago Press.

8. Popenoe, D., & Whitehead, B. D. (1999). *Should we live together? What young adults need to know about cohabitation before marriage.* New Brunswick, NJ: National Marriage Project.

9. Axinn, W. G., & Barber, J. S. (1997). Living arrangements and family formation attitudes in early adulthood. *Journal of Marriage and the Family, 59,* 595–611.

10. Kahn, J. R., & London, K. A. (1991). Premarital sex and the risk of divorce. *Journal of Marriage and the Family, 53,* 845–855.

11. Lye, D. N., & Biblarz, T. J. (1990). *The effects of attitudes towards family life and roles on marital satisfaction.* Paper presented at the annual meeting of the Population Association of America, Toronto.

12. Kahn & London, Premarital sex and the risk of divorce, p. 847.

13. Kahn & London, Premarital sex and the risk of divorce.

14. Newcomb, M. D., & Bentler, D. M. (1981). Marital breakdown. In S. Duck & R. Gilmour (Eds.), *Personal relationships, Volume 3. Personal relationships in disorder* (pp. 57–94). New York: Academic Press.

15. Kurdek, L. A. (1991). Marital stability and changes in marital quality in newly wed couples: A test of the contextual model. *Journal of Social and Personal Relationships, 8,* 27–48.

16. Stephan, T. D. (1985). Fixed-sequence and circular-causal models of relationship development: Divergent views on the role of communication in intimacy. *Journal of Marriage and the Family, 47,* 955–963.

17. Miller, S., Miller, P., Nunnally, E. W., & Wackman, D. B. (1991). *Talking and listening together.* Littleton, CO: Interpersonal Communication Programs.

18. Joanning, Brewster, & Koval, The communication rapid assessment scale.

19. Rusbult, C. E., & Zembrodt, I. M. (1983). Responses to dissatisfaction in romantic involvements: A multidimensional scaling analysis. *Journal of Experimental Social Psychology, 19,* 274–293.

20. Rusbult, Johnson, & Morrow, Impact of couple patterns of problem solving. . . .

Chapter 7

1. Gordon, S. (1988). *Why love is not enough.* Boston: Bob Adams.

2. Washton, A., & Boundy, D. (1989). *Willpower's not enough: Understanding and recovering from addictions of every kind.* New York: Harper Perennial.

Chapter 8

1. Coalition for Marriage, Family, and Couples Education. (1998). *1998 Directory of Youth and School-Based Marriage Education Programs.* Washington, DC: CMFCE.

The Author

Jeffry H. Larson, Ph.D., LMFT, CLFE, is a professor and program chairman of the Marriage and Family Therapy Programs in the School of Family Life at Brigham Young University in Provo, Utah. He has a B.A. (1971) and an M.A. (1974) in psychology from Brigham Young University and a Ph.D. in marriage and family therapy from Texas Tech University (1980). Dr. Larson has twenty years of experience conducting premarital counseling and marriage therapy and has taught marriage preparation, marriage enhancement, and marital therapy courses at four different major universities. Dr. Larson's research has focused on premarital predictors of marital satisfaction, the assessment of readiness for marriage, and the development of premarital education programs. He has published over forty articles in major professional journals and is coauthor (with Dr. Tom Holman) of a new academic book on premarital prediction research, *Premarital Prediction of Marital Quality or Breakup* (in press).

Dr. Larson served as chairperson of the Marriage Preparation Focus Group of the National Council on Family Relations, is a Licensed Marriage and Family Therapist, and a Certified Family Life Educator. In addition, he is a Clinical Member and Approved Supervisor in the American Association for Marriage and Family Therapy and serves as a member of the Utah State Licensing Board for Marriage and Family Therapy.

Dr. Larson presents workshops nationally and locally on how to predict marital satisfaction before marriage, myths about marriage and mate selection, and marriage preparation. He has appeared nationally on the *Good Morning America* news program and local television and radio stations.

ML